ROUGH
GUIDES

T0086100

POCKET **ROUGH GUIDE**
REYKJAVÍK

written and researched by
DAVID LEFFMAN AND JAMES PROCTOR
updated by
JOANNA REEVES

CONTENTS

REYKJAVÍK

If you're more used to the traffic-clogged streets of other major European cities, Reykjavík's sense of space and calm will come as a breath of fresh air. That said, the world's most northerly capital still dwarfs Iceland's other built-up areas, with the Greater Reykjavík area home to two out of every three Icelanders. The atmosphere generated by this bustling port, with its highbrow museums, colourful streets and buzzing nightlife, has earned the city a reputation for hedonistic revelry which draws visitors from across the globe, in record-breaking numbers – and its popularity shows no signs of waning.

Hallgrímskirkja, the largest church in Iceland

The natural spectacle of the Northern Lights over Reykjavík

Split roughly into two halves by the brilliant waters of Tjörnin lake, the tiny city centre is more a place to amble around and take in the suburban-looking streets and corner cafés than somewhere to hurtle about, ticking off attractions. Reykjavík lacks the grand and imposing buildings found in other Nordic capitals, possessing instead apparently ramshackle clusters of houses, either clad in garishly painted corrugated iron or daubed in pebbledash as protection against the ferocious North Atlantic storms. This rather unkempt feel, though, is as much part of the city's charm as the views across the sea to glaciers and the sheer mountains that form the backdrop to the streets. Even in the heart of this capital, nature is always in evidence – there can be few other cities in the world, for example, where greylag geese regularly overfly the busy centre, sending bemused visitors, more accustomed to pigeons, scurrying for cover.

In the midst of the essentially residential city centre, it is the

When to visit

Icelandic weather is notoriously unpredictable. In summer, Reykjavík tends to be cloudy and showery, though there can be long, clear spells of sunny weather, too. However, one thing is consistent – it's never really warm. Summer in Reykjavík is more about the long daylight hours than a sudden surge in temperature – the average summer range in the city is 8–14°C. Since Reykjavík lies south of the Arctic Circle, it doesn't experience true Midnight Sun, though nights are light from mid-May to early August. Conversely, in winter, days are short and dark – at the shortest time of the year, in December, the sun doesn't rise until around 10.30–11am, setting again just a couple of hours later. Between September and January, there's a good chance of seeing the Northern Lights. During winter, storms are frequent, and temperatures tend to hover a few degrees either side of freezing point.

Best places to swim

Reykjavík has several excellent swimming pools to choose from. The biggest is Laugardalslaug, with outdoor pools and hot pots (see page 71). Following extension work in 2017, Sundhöllin (see page 124) now boasts a large new outdoor pool, in addition to its exisiting indoor one. It also has hot pots and sun terraces. Most visitors can't wait to try the geothermal hot pots and sea lagoon at Nauthólsvík, where there's also a glorious sandy beach (see page 66). The latest addition to the hot spring scene, the steam-shrouded Sky Lagoon (see page 77) opened in 2021, with a geothermal water-fed spa and infinity pool. Wherever you swim, you must shower thoroughly without a swimming costume before entering the water, since it is not treated with chlorine.

Hallgrímskirkja, a gargantuan white concrete church towering over the surrounding houses, that is the most enduring image of Reykjavík. Below this, the elegant shops and stylish bars and restaurants that line the main street and commercial thoroughfare of Laugavegur are a consumer's heaven. The central core of streets around Laugavegur and Skólavörðustígur is where you'll find a range of engaging museums, too. The displays in the Landnámssýning and the Saga Museum, for example, offer an accessible introduction to Iceland's stirring past; while whale-watching and puffin-spotting tours from the city harbour give you a chance to experience Icelandic nature up close.

If you have some time to spare, it's well worth venturing outside the city limits to explore some of southwest Iceland's greatest attractions. Top of everyone's list is the erupting geyser known as Strokkur, plus the nearby rift valley, Þingvellir, where you can see a clear split in the earth's tectonic plates; both are easily accessible on day-trips from the capital. A little further afield, the Westman Islands, scene of the famous 1973 volcanic eruption, beckon enticingly, while the rugged natural beauty of Þorsmörk national park and the Landmannalaugar geothermal springs – which mark the jumping-off point into Iceland's remote and uninhabited Interior – are equally worthy of your time.

Sky Lagoon in Kópavogur

Where to...

Shop

Reykjavík's main thoroughfare, Laugavegur, and the Kringlan shopping centre are where you'll find most of the city's **shops**, though Skólavörðustígur has ramped up its act in recent years. Remember that most goods are available at tax-free prices when exported from Iceland – ask in store when browsing for details of the cash refund (see page 129). Particularly good-value purchases include anything made of **wool** – from traditional sweaters, gloves and scarves to blankets, shawls and hats. Think carefully about where you spend your money: support local and look out for official quality label Vakinn when buying souvenirs.
OUR FAVOURITES: Kolaportið, see page 37; Ióa, see page 50; Víkurprjón, see page 101.

Eat

The one thing every visitor remembers about a visit to Reykjavík is eating the freshest **fish** they have ever tasted. In fact, many Icelanders simply refuse to order fish when they travel abroad, because it doesn't taste like it does at home. Reykjavík's abundant fish restaurants serve unusual options such as catfish and blue ling alongside more common species like cod and haddock. A crop of New Nordic restaurants is springing up across the city, many scooping **Michelin stars** for their culinary credentials, helmed by creative young chefs giving an inventive twist to traditional recipes. Look out for lunchtime specials (often set menus) for bargain prices.
OUR FAVOURITES: Sümac, see page 59; Dill, see page 57; ÓX, see page 58.

Drink

Drinking in Reykjavík is expensive. However, there are several ways to cut costs. Consider buying wine, beer or spirits on arrival, at the duty-free store inside Keflavík airport. Ask the helpful staff about your duty-free allowances. Alternatively, buy your booze from the **state-run alcohol stores**, *vínbúðin* (see pages 30 and 75), dotted across the city, where prices are higher than at duty free but less than in bars and restaurants. Of course, having a drink in a bar is also tempting – for a wallet-friendly option, look out for happy hours when prices on alcohol are slashed.
OUR FAVOURITES: Micro Bar, see page 59; SKÝ Bar, see page 45; Bravó, see page 59.

Go out

Reykjavík is deservedly known for its **nightlife**. Although the scene is actually no bigger than that of any small-sized town in most other countries, what sets it apart is the northerly setting and location for all this revelry – during summer, it's very disorientating to enter a club in the small hours with the sun just about to set, only to emerge a couple of hours later into the blinding daylight of the Icelandic morning. The **bars and clubs** of Austurstræti, Hafnarstræti and Laugavegur are the liveliest in the city. It can be fun to join in when clubbers spill out into Lækjartorg early on Sunday morning for an alfresco end to the night.
OUR FAVOURITES: Kaffibarinn, see page 65; Gaukurinn, see page 39; Hverfisbarinn, see page 59.

Reykjavík at a glance

The harbour p.40.
Busy with fishing trawlers and whaling ships, the harbour area boasts some fine cultural venues, too.

Aðalstræti, Hafnarstræti and Tryggvagata p.32.
This hub of bars and shops also includes a couple of museums – perfect wandering territory.

Lækjartorg, Austurstræti and Austurvöllur p.26.
The urban core of Reykjavík, with two of its main squares, is full of locals just hanging out.

Tjörnin and around p.46.
A circuit of this peaceful lake at the heart of the city guarantees picture-postcard views.

Öskjuhlíð and around p.66.
This wooded hill, where Reykjavíkers come to walk, cycle, jog and picnic, is also home to one of the city's iconic buildings.

Whales of Iceland

Harpa

Ráðhúsið (City Hall)

Þjóðminjasafn (National Museum)

Hallgrím

Háskóli Íslands

Háskólabíó Cinema

Norræna húsið

Reykjavik City Airport

Nauthólsv geotherm lagoon

Sky Lagoon

KÓPAVOGUR

Viðey

Bankastræti and around p.52.
Home to Reykjavík's main commercial artery and a number of fine historical buildings.

Hallgrímskirkja and around p.60.
The city's landmark building is a modernist triumph – and there are other sculptural highlights in the area, too.

Viðey Ferry Terminal

Sigurjón Ólafsson Museum

SÆBRAUT

Höfði

SÆBRAUT

Laugardalslaug

Laugardalsvöllur

Ásmundursafn

Botanical Garden

Laugardalshöll

MÚLINN

Húsdýragarðurinn

Fjölskyldu-garðurinn

arvalsstaðir

LABRAUT

Kringlan shopping centre

MIKLABRAUT

City Theatre

Eastern Reykjavík p.70.
A sporty corner of town, with its largest sports stadium and principal swimming pool.

Things not to miss

It's not possible to see everything that Reykjavík has to offer in one trip – and we don't suggest you try. What follows is a selective taste of the city's highlights, from engaging museums to elemental landscapes.

∧ **Sky Lagoon**
See page 77
Wallow in Iceland's latest
newcomer to the geothermal spa
scene, taking in views of the North
Atlantic from the infinity pool.
Try the seven-stage cleansing
treatment for silky-smooth skin.

> **Strokkur**
See page 90
The erupting geyser that
everyone wants to see – the
mighty Strokkur shoots a huge
spout of boiling water 30m into
the air every few minutes.

< **The view from
Hallgrímskirkja tower**
See page 60
The classic vista of Reykjavík, with
the city's jumble of multicoloured
buildings unfurling beneath you.

‹ Þingvellir
See page 86
See the sheer-sided rift valley where the Eurasian and North American tectonic plates are literally tearing apart; the belly of the valley yawns 4km wide between 40m-high basalt walls.

∨ Gullfoss
See page 90
One of the most popular tourist attractions in Iceland, the Hvítá cascades down a three-step staircase before plunging, in two more stages, into a deep crevice.

< **Harpa**
See page 43
Unsurpassed views of the harbour area unfold from the top floor of Reykjavík's landmark opera house, whose glass-clad architecture cuts a dramatic figure on the waterfront.

∨ **Seljalandsfoss**
See page 95
Footpaths thread behind the thundering curtain of water at Seljalandsfoss, giving a breathtaking perspective of the waterfalls and mist-shrouded landscape beyond.

∧ Þjóðminjasafn
See page 47

The examples of medieval church art inside the National Museum are some of Iceland's finest treasures; a highlight is the carved church door from Valþjófsstaður in Fljótsdalur, dating from around 1200.

< Whale watching
See page 43

Regular boat tours depart from the city harbour throughout the year, sailing for Faxaflói bay north of Reykjavík to spot whales; you're also likely to see white beaked dolphins and harbour porpoises.

∧ Blue Lagoon
See page 80
Lolling around in the milky-blue, silica-rich waters at Iceland's premier thermal spa is not just relaxing – it's also extremely good for your skin.

∨ Saga Museum
See page 40
At Reykjavík's answer to Madame Tussauds, come face to face with the main characters of the Sagas – and even sample the smells of the Viking period.

∧ **Horseriding**
See page 125
With their fifth gait – a cross
between a trot and a canter, called
tölt – Icelandic horses can move
smoothly across the island's
rough terrain.

< **Landnámssýning**
See page 33
Discover how Reykjavík's
first settlers lived and see the
extensive remains of a tenth-
century Viking hall.

< **Skógarfoss**
See page 98
A drop of over 60m makes this waterfall one of the most impressive in southern Iceland – particularly when the roaring waters and fine spray are viewed from the riverbed.

∨ **Laugardalslaug**
See page 71
Iceland's biggest and best swimming pool is a Reykjavík institution. There's a 50m outdoor pool, plus smaller children's pools, as well as several hot pots.

THINGS NOT TO MISS

Day one in Reykjavík

Whales of Iceland. See page 41. Begin the day checking out the life-size, silicone models of the whales found in Icelandic waters and learn all about these giants of the sea.

Whale watching. See page 43. Head down to the harbour and go in search of the real thing – humpback whales are the most likely to show – on a whale-watching boat tour just off the Reykjavík coast.

Lunch. See page 30. An easy walk from the harbour, *Apótek* serves a good-value fishy lunch, amid a beautifully appointed interior.

Whales of Iceland

Þjóðminjasafn. See page 47. Get to grips with Iceland's stirring past at the National Museum, whose exhibitions on Viking graves, medieval church art and DNA testing are first class.

Tjörnin. See page 46. From the National Museum, take a pleasant stroll back into the city centre along the banks of Tjörnin lake, for some great views of Reykjavík and its birdlife.

Hallgrímskirkja. See page 60. Ride the lift to the top of the Hallgrímskirkja's tower for superlative views of the city and coastline, then check out the huge church organ.

Apótek

Sundhöllin. See page 124. From the church, walk down to Sundhöllin swimming pool, where you can swim, wallow in the hot pots, or even sunbathe on the sun terraces if the weather allows.

Dinner. See page 64. Refuel on traditional Icelandic eats, like meat soup or a herring plate, at *Café Loki*; nab a table upstairs for excellent views over Hallgrímskirkja.

Hallgrímskirkja

Day two in Reykjavík

Landnámssýning. See page 33. Inspect the remains of a Viking-age hall, still in its original location, and learn all about the days of the Settlement in this informative and engaging museum.

Saga Museum. See page 40. Put faces to some of the names who featured prominently during the Settlement of Iceland – the wax models in this museum are startlingly lifelike.

🍴 **Lunch.** See page 44. Head to the waterfront to eat some of the freshest fish you're ever likely to taste at locals' favourite, *Fish & Chips Vagninn*.

Saga Museum

Marshall House. See page 42. Get your culture fix at this ahead-of-the-curve gallery space and Olafur Eliasson's artist studio.

Laugavegur. See page 55. Time for some retail therapy: go for a wander along the length of Laugavegur and you might just succumb to the range of goods on offer.

Phallological Museum. See page 61. At the eastern end of Laugavegur, you'll find Reykjavík's most offbeat museum – dedicated to the humble penis. Examples of members from every mammal species found in Iceland (human included) abound.

Laugavegur

🍴 **Dinner.** See page 45. Classic Icelandic dishes are given a modern makeover at *Matur og Drykkur*, next to the Saga Museum.

Seafront stroll. See page 61. Take a post-dinner amble along Sæbraut for great views of Mount Esja, as well as a chance to see the iconic *Sólfar* statue and historic Höfði house, watched over by the 2019-built Höfði lighthouse.

Matur og Drykkur

Away from the crowds

Reykjavík is one of Europe's smaller and saner capitals. Escaping the crowds and finding a spot of peace and tranquillity is relatively easy.

Hafnarfjörður. See page 76. Hop on the bus for the short ride to Hafnarfjörður, Reykjavík's southern neighbour. In comparison with the capital, the streets here are all but empty of visitors.

Víðey. See page 74. For just 1100kr you can ride the ferry to Víðey for great views of Reykjavík and the surrounding coastline. Though fairly small, Víðey boasts some great hiking trails, too, offering a real chance to commune with nature in the city.

Víðey

Reykjanes Peninsula. See page 80. With your own transport a drive around the southwestern point of the Reykjanes Peninsula, through the lava landscapes between Grindavík and Hafnir, is especially rewarding – not least for an intercontinental bridge, steaming mud pools, and sea cliffs stacked with bird life.

Öskjuhlíð. See page 66. The forested slopes of this city park south of the centre are the perfect place to escape the crowds. Pack a picnic and find your own shady glade among the trees.

Reykjanes Peninsula

South of Hallgrímskirkja. See page 60. The streets south of Hallgrímskirkja, notably Njarðargata, Baldursgata and Óðinsgata, are relatively unexplored by visitors to the city. A stroll here is a chance to see residential Reykjavík – look for a few older houses weatherproofed in corrugated iron.

Sun terraces, Sundhöllin. See page 124. Sheltered from the wind, the outdoor terraces at the swimming pool here are a wonderful spot to catch the rays (in the buff) on a warm day – and they're little known to visitors.

South of Hallgrímskirkja

Eat and drink like a local

With a wide range of eating and drinking options in the Icelandic capital, it can be hard to make a sound choice. Here, then, is how the locals do it.

Vínbúðin. See pages 30 and 75. Given the high price of alcohol in Reykjavík's bars and restaurants, many locals drink at home instead. Buy your booze from the *vínbúðin* on Austurstræti and save a small fortune.

Mokka. See page 65. This simple café on Skólavörðustígur is a Reykjavík classic. It's been plying the people of the city with caffeine for years – and they can't get enough of it.

Frú Lauga. See page 64. Drop into this popular foodie shop to pick up some market-fresh produce for a picnic lunch – you'll feel like you've lived in Reykjavík for years.

Mokka

Happy hours. See pages 45 and 65. Save money by drinking during the happy hours which are posted up outside many bars. A large beer can go for as little as 600kr – much less than you'd pay at home.

Grandi Mathöll. See page 44. A hip gourmand hall packed with Asian fusion street food trucks, giving a Korean or Vietnamese twist to Icelandic fish and seafood.

Sandholt. See page 59. Reykjavíkers claim this is the best café in the city. There's a great choice of takeaway pastries and sandwiches and its home-made chocolates are famous.

Bæjarins Beztu Pylsur

Bæjarins Beztu Pylsur. See page 38. Legendary mobile stand down near the harbourfront, which has been serving loyal customers its trademark hot dogs smothered in fried onions and lashings of remoulade since 1937.

Kaffivagninn. See page 44. For great cakes and breakfasts, head to this harbourside fishermen's hangout, one of Reykjavík's oldest cafés.

Sandholt

Kids' Reykjavík

Despite its small size, Reykjavík is a very child-friendly city, and whatever the weather, there's always something going on nearby to help keep children entertained.

Blue Lagoon. See page 80. The iconic Icelandic spa. This huge spread of milky-blue, steaming water sits among the Reykjanes Peninsula's lunar landscape of black volcanic rubble, ideal for letting off steam going to, or from, the airport.

Whale watching. See page 43. Whale-watching tours depart Reykjavík harbour throughout the year, with a fairly decent chance of seeing minke whales, white beaked dolphins and harbour porpoises – not to mention puffins and other sea birds.

Viðey trip. See page 74. A brief ferry ride from Sundahöfn harbour will land you on this extinct volcano. Though little remains of the island's rich history, it's a great place to ramble along easy coastal tracks, enjoying the seascapes.

Horseriding. See page 125. Icelandic horses are a unique breed, known for their stocky build, quiet temper and gliding *tölt* gait. Farms outside Reykjavík organize treks for all levels of riding experience, lasting from an hour to a day.

Saga Museum. See page 40. Lively waxworks illustrating key figures from the country's early history – don't miss Hrafna-Flóki, discoverer of Iceland, or the Viking-poet Egil Skallagrímsson – though be aware that some scenes are realistically brutal.

Tjörnin. See page 46. Head for the corner with Fríkirkjuvegur where graylag geese, eider ducks and even whooper swans gather, hoping for handouts. Don't miss the amazing relief map of Iceland, which fills its own room inside the nearby Ráðhúsið.

Blue Lagoon

Whale watching

Tjörnin

Out of town

Enhance even a brief trip to Reykjavík with some raw, iconic Icelandic scenery, all within an easy hour or two's drive of the capital.

Golden Circle. See page 86. Classic Icelandic trio: a thundering two-tier cataract through a gorge at Gulfoss; Geysir's erupting hot springs; and the stunning Þingvellir rift valley, historic setting for Iceland's original parliament, where the country is literally tearing apart.

Heimaey. See page 100. This small island – home to a few thousand people and millions of seabirds – remains actively volcanic after a devastating eruption during the 1970s. Climb to the still-steaming crater rim of the Eldfell volcano for fantastic views.

Heimaey

Seljalandsfoss. See page 95. One of Iceland's most beautiful waterfalls, this thin ribbon cascades off a plateau's edge into a broad plunge pool. Walk around behind the curtain for unique views – and a good soaking.

Vík. See page 99. Iceland's only coastal town without a harbour, charming Vík sports a black volcanic sand beach, the offshore "Troll Rocks", and a looming, grassy headland thick with roosting seabird colonies.

Vík

Reynishverfi. See page 99. Attractive shingle beach near Iceland's southernmost point, with beautiful seascapes, basalt rock formations in nearby cliffs and resident puffins through the summer. Just be sure to take care with the dangerous surf.

Sólheimajökull. See page 98. One of the closest glaciers to Reykjavík, and the most accessible, where you can approach the blackened, gravel-covered snout and even try your hand at some ice-climbing (under the watchful eye of a guide).

Sólheimajökull

PLACES

Harpa

Lækjartorg, Austurstræti and Austurvöllur

The best place to get your first taste of Reykjavík is around Lækjartorg and the adjoining pedestrianized Austurstræti, on the square's western side. This area is a lively meeting place for Reykjavík's urbanites, where locals come to stroll, strut and sit on benches munching cakes, ice creams and burgers bought from the nearby fast-food outlets and the 10–11 supermarket. If Reykjavík has a main square, meanwhile, it is Austurvöllur, a more stately – though still diminutive – space south of Austurstræti that is home to the Icelandic parliament, Reykjavík cathedral and a handful of imposing buildings, including the city's very first hotel, *Hótel Borg*, dating from the 1930s.

Lækjartorg

MAP PAGE 28, POCKET MAP D4

Lækjartorg square has always been at the heart of Reykjavík life; indeed, it was here that farmers bringing produce to market ended their long journey from the surrounding countryside and set up camp to sell their goods. Although the Icelandic name does indeed mean "square" ("brook square", in fact, named after the stream that flows beneath it), Lækjartorg is

Austurvöllur, a flower-lined square popular with city workers

Icelandic people power

Every Saturday between October 2008 and January 2009, thousands of Icelanders gathered in Austurvöllur to voice their anger over the collapse of the Icelandic banking system which, it's estimated, left one in five families bankrupt. The protesters burned the flag of Landsbanki (one of the country's leading banks) and were soon calling for heads to roll. The main target of popular discontent was the leader of the Icelandic Central Bank and former long-serving politician, Davið Oddsson, who was squarely blamed for the economic collapse, and was replaced in March 2009. The demonstrators became more vocal at the lack of decisive government action and finally, after three and a half months of protests in Austurvöllur and at various locations around the country, Prime Minister Geir Haarde admitted defeat; to national jubilation, his administration fell on January 26, 2009. Today, thanks to the square's central position and the fact that MPs regularly trot through Austurvöllur on their way to parliamentary sessions, this remains Iceland's favourite place to harangue the government.

not the kind of grand, imposing place you might find elsewhere in Europe: it is more a wide, paved pedestrian entrance to Austurstræti.

Despite its relatively modest appearance, however, this can be one of the most boisterous corners of the city. On Friday and Saturday evenings, particularly during summertime, hundreds of revellers fill the square when the clubs empty out at around 4 or 5am, jostling for prime position – the noise from the good-hearted throng can be deafening.

Austurstræti

MAP PAGE 28, POCKET MAP D4

By day, **Austurstræti** has a busy commercial air as people dash in and out of the post office, pop in to the Eymundsson bookshop and sort out money matters at the main branch of Landsbanki. Beyond its junction with Pósthússtræti, the road gives itself over solely to pleasure, as this is where some of the city's best bars and restaurants can be found. Austurstræti is also the location for the *vínbúð* **state alcohol store**, a futuristic glass-and-steel structure at number 10a,

where those who want to drink at home buy their booze.

Austurvöllur

MAP PAGE 28, POCKET MAP C4

Pósthússtræti, running south from Austurstræti, leads into another small square, **Austurvöllur**, a favourite place for city slickers from nearby offices to catch a few rays during their lunch breaks, stretched out on the flower-lined grassy lawns. The square's modest proportions and nondescript apartment blocks, meanwhile, somewhat belie its historical importance: this was the site of the farm of Reykjavík's first settler, **Ingólfur Arnarson**; it's thought he grew his hay on the land where the square now stands, and it marks the original core of the city.

Similarly, the central, elevated statue of the nineteenth-century independence campaigner **Jón Sigurðsson**, entitled *The Pride of Iceland, its Sword and Shield*, faces two of the most important buildings in the country – the Alþingishúsið and the Dómkirkjan – though you'd never realize their status from their appearance.

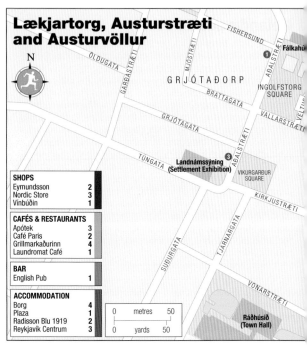

Lækjartorg, Austurstræti and Austurvöllur

N

GRJÓTAÐORP

INGOLFSTORG SQUARE

Landnámssýning ③
(Settlement Exhibition)

VIKURGARÐUR SQUARE

KIRKJUSTRÆTI

SHOPS	
Eymundsson	2
Nordic Store	3
Vínbúðin	1

CAFÉS & RESTAURANTS	
Apótek	3
Café Paris	2
Grillmarkaðurinn	4
Laundromat Café	1

BAR	
English Pub	1

ACCOMMODATION	
Borg	4
Plaza	1
Radisson Blu 1919	2
Reykjavík Centrum	3

0	metres	50
0	yards	50

Ráðhúsið
(Town Hall)

Alþingishúsið (Parliament House)

MAP PAGE 28, POCKET MAP C4
Austurvöllur Square. Closed to the public.

The **Alþingishúsið** is ordinary in the extreme, a slight building made of grey basalt quarried from nearby Skólavörðuholt hill, with the date of its completion (1881) etched into its dark frontage – yet this unremarkable structure played a pivotal role in bringing about Icelandic independence. In 1798, the parliament moved to Reykjavík from Þingvellir (see page 86), where it had been operating virtually without interruption since 930 AD. Within just two years, however, it was dissolved as Danish power reached its peak. Yet after much struggle, the Alþingi regained its powers from Copenhagen as a consultative body in 1843, and a constitution was granted in 1874 that

made Iceland self-governing in domestic affairs. The **Act of Union**, passed in this building in 1918, made Iceland a sovereign state under the Danish Crown, but by 1940 Denmark was occupied by the Nazis and the Alþingi had assumed the duties normally carried out by the monarch, declaring its intention to dissolve the Act of Union at the end of the war. Today, the modest interior, illuminated by chandeliers, more resembles a town council chamber than the seat of a national parliament.

Dómkirkjan

MAP PAGE 28, POCKET MAP D4
Lækjargata 14a. Free.

Reykjavík's Lutheran cathedral, the **Dómkirkjan**, is a Neoclassical stone structure partly shrouded in corrugated iron to protect it from the weather. It was built between

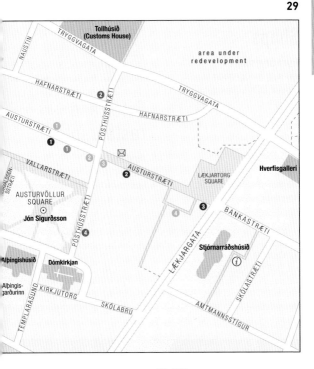

1787 and 1796 after Christian VII of Denmark scrapped the Catholic bishoprics of Hólar in the north and Skálholt in the south, in favour of a Lutheran diocese in what was fast growing into Iceland's main centre of population. The church may be plain on the outside, but its unassuming facade conceals a beautiful interior: a series of perfectly designed arched windows punctuates the unadorned white-painted walls, giving an impression of complete architectural harmony. The cathedral is now deemed too small for great gatherings and services of state, and the roomier Hallgrímskirkja (see page 60) is preferred for state funerals and other such well-attended functions, although the **opening of parliament** is still marked with a church service in the Dómkirkjan.

Dómkirkjan

Shops

Eymundsson

MAP PAGE 28, POCKET MAP D4
Austurstræti 18 Ⓦ penninn.is.
The best bookshop in Reykjavík,
with a broad selection of English
titles about Iceland plus stationery,
postcards and other souvenirs.

Nordic Store

MAP PAGE 28, POCKET MAP D4
Lækjargata 2 Ⓦ nordicstore.net.
A one-stop shop for all things
woollen, including cosy Icelandic
jumpers. Eiderdown duvets are also
available, and shipping is available.

Vínbúðin

MAP PAGE 28, POCKET MAP C4
Austurstræti 10a Ⓦ vinbudin.is.
A handily located branch of
the state alcohol monopoly.

Remember that, in Iceland,
booze is sold exclusively at
vínbúðin – you'll search in vain
elsewhere or spend a small
fortune to drink with meals.

Cafés and restaurants

Apótek

MAP PAGE 28, POCKET MAP D4
Austurstræti 16 Ⓦ apotekrestaurant.is.
Apótek, once Reykjavík's
main apothecary, has been
reimagined as a stylish restaurant
specializing in fresh seafood with
a modern twist. The set lunches
(6990Kr for two courses,
7990Kr for three) represent a
pretty good deal. Wide choice of
wine, too, with bottles lining the
wall-hung shelves. KrKrKrKr

Grillmarkaðurinn

Café Paris

Café Paris

MAP PAGE 28, POCKET MAP D4

Austurstræti 14 Ⓦ **cafeparis.is.**

Long gone are the days when
this was virtually the only café
in town. Since it opened in
1992, the French-style *Café Paris*
has become a Reykjavík fixture,
with outdoor seating overlooking
the Alþingi in summer. Offers
a decent selection of brunches,
as well as excellent crêpes and
refreshing salads. The weekday
lunch special features catch of
the day at a bargainous 2990Kr.
KrKrKrKr

Grillmarkaðurinn

MAP PAGE 28, POCKET MAP D4

Lækjargata 2a Ⓦ **grillmarkadurinn.is.**

Everything served at this stylish
modern restaurant – from
salmon and cod to steaks,
burgers and vegetables – is
sourced from local farmers and
fishermen and cooked on the
custom-made charcoal grill.
KrKrKrKr

Laundromat Café

MAP PAGE 28, POCKET MAP C3

Austurstræti 9 Ⓦ **thelaundromatcafe.com.**

The walls of this café are covered
with maps and the bar is made of
bookshelves lined with paperbacks.
On the wallet-friendly menu
are burgers, salads, soups and
sandwiches, plus breakfast options.
Oh, and there's a laundry on site,
too, of course. Kr

Bar

English Pub

MAP PAGE 28, POCKET MAP D4

Austurstræti 12 Ⓦ **enskibarinn.is.**

This is an attempt to create a
British-style pub in the heart of
Reykjavík, and while the interior
is none too genuine, there's
lager, Guinness and Kilkenny on
draught, lots of footie on TV and
live music at the weekend. You
can also try spinning the "wheel of
fortune", with up to eight free beers
as the prize if you win.

Aðalstræti, Hafnarstræti and Tryggvagata

The trio of streets, Aðalstræti, Hafnarstræti and Tryggvagata, contains many of Reykjavík's bars and tourist-oriented shops. Don't confuse them, though, with the grand boulevards you might find in other capital cities; instead, they're modest affairs, barely a couple of hundred metres in length. Although they can't compete with Laugavegur, the city's main shopping street (see page 55), which is an altogether busier thoroughfare, these three are arguably a more pleasant place to stroll and linger. You'll doubtless end up spending time here sampling the shopping scene and dipping into the bar culture or passing through on your way to the harbour. It's also where you'll find a couple of the city's museums, which come as a welcome addition to Reykjavík's cultural scene.

Aðalstræti

MAP PAGE 34, POCKET MAP C4

From the southwestern corner of Austurvöllur, Kirkjustræti runs the short distance to Reykjavík's oldest street, **Aðalstræti**, which

Landnámssýning (Settlement Exhibition)

traces the route taken in the late ninth century by Ingólfur Arnarson (see page 131) from his farm at the southern end down to the sea. In addition to the remains of a Viking-age farmhouse on display inside the Landnámssýning museum, Aðalstræti also holds Reykjavík's **oldest surviving building**, a squat timber structure at no. 10. It dates back to 1752, and has served as a weaving shed, a bishop's residence and the home of Skúli Magnússon, High Sheriff of Iceland, who encouraged the development of craft industries here. It is now part of the Reykjavík City Museum and is an extension of the Settlement Exhibition (see page 33), connected via an underground passage. On the opposite side of the street, a few steps north towards the sea outside the present no. 9, is Ingólfur Arnarson's freshwater well, **Ingólfsbrunnur**, which was discovered by fluke during road repairs here in 1992 and is now glassed over for posterity.

Aðalstræti 10, Reykjavík's oldest surviving building

Landnámssýning (Settlement Exhibition)

MAP PAGE 34, POCKET MAP C4

Aðalstræti 16 ⓦ reykjavikcitymuseum.is/ the-settlement-exhibition. Charge.

The **Landnámssýning**, whose centrepiece is the extensive ruins of a **Viking-age farmhouse**, is one of Reykjavík's most remarkable museums. Housed in a purpose-built hall directly beneath Aðalstræti, the structure's oval-shaped stone walls, excavated in 2001, enclose a sizeable living space of 85 square metres, with a central hearth as the focal point. Dating the farmhouse has been quite straightforward, since the layer of volcanic ash that fell across Iceland following a powerful eruption in around 871 AD lies just beneath the building; it's estimated, therefore, that people lived here between 930 and 1000 AD. The exhibition's wall space is given over to panoramic views of forest and scrubland to convey a realistic impression of what Reykjavík would have looked like at the time of the Settlement. Indeed, when the

first settlers arrived in the area, the hills were covered in birch woods. However, just one hundred years later, the birch had all but disappeared, felled to make way for grazing land or burnt for charcoal needed for iron-smelting. An underground passage connects the farmhouse to an exhibition hall in Reykjavík's oldest building, at Aðalstræti 10, which is included in the ticket price.

Hafnarstræti

MAP PAGE 34, POCKET MAP D3

Many of the buildings on the south side of **Hafnarstræti** were formerly owned by Danish merchants during the 1602–1855 Trade Monopoly. Indeed, this street, as its name suggests (*hafnar* means "harbour"), once bordered the sea and gave access to the harbour, the city's economic lifeline and means of contact with the outside world. Today, Hafnarstræti is several blocks from the ocean, after landfill extended the city foreshore, and is home to a clutch of excellent

SHOPS
Fischersund 2
Kolaportið 1
The Viking 3

CAFÉS & RESTAURANTS
Bæjarins Beztu Pylsur 4
BRÚT Restaurant 3
Fish Market 7
Grillhúsið 2
Hornið 6
Kaffi Ó-le 5
Reykjavík Fish Restaurant 1

BARS
Dubliner 3
Frederiksen Ale House 2
Gaukurinn 1

Aðalstræti,
Hafnarstræti
and Tryggvagata

bars and restaurants. Together with Austurstræti to the south and Tryggvagata to the north, it forms part of a rectangular block of cafés, restaurants and drinking holes that are well worth exploring.

Fálkahúsið

MAP PAGE 34, POCKET MAP C3
Corner of Aðalstræti and Hafnarstræti.
Opposite the tourist office, and covered in corrugated iron for protection, **Fálkahúsið** is another of Reykjavík's beautifully restored timber buildings, one of three in the city where the King of Denmark once kept his much-prized Icelandic falcons. Its turret-like side walls and sheer size still impress, especially when you consider the huge amount of timber that was imported for the job, as Iceland had no trees of its own. Cast an eye to the

roof and you'll spot two carved wooden falcons still keeping guard over the building.

Tryggvagata

MAP PAGE 34, POCKET MAP D3
Tryggvagata, one block north of the bustle of Hafnarstræti, is remarkable for a few things other than the number of consonants in its name. The imposing, multicoloured mosaic **mural** by Gerður Helgadóttir (1928–75) close to its junction with Pósthússtræti portrays a busy harbour scene, complete with fishing trawlers and cranes, and livens up the otherwise dull Tollhúsið (Customs House). At the time of writing, the street beneath the art-splashed facade was closed as works were underway to transform a carpark into a pedestrianized square. Also along here are Ljósmindasafn – Reykjavík's

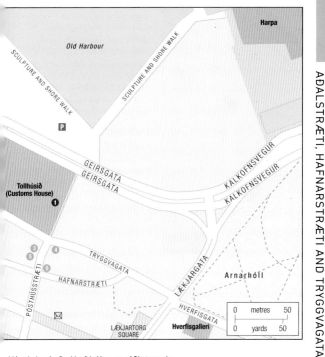

Harpa

Old Harbour

SCULPTURE AND SHORE WALK

SCULPTURE AND SHORE WALK

P

GEIRSGATA
GEIRSGATA

KALKOFNSVEGUR
KALKOFNSVEGUR

Tollhúsið
(Customs House)
❶

③
⑤ ④
⑥

TRYGGVAGATA

PÓSTHÚSSTRÆTI

HAFNARSTRÆTI

LÆKJARGATA

Arnarhóll

HVERFISGATA

LÆKJARTORG
SQUARE

Hverfisgalleri

| 0 | metres | 50 |
| 0 | yards | 50 |

Ljósmindasafn, Reykjavík's Museum of Photography

Hafnarhúsið, (Harbour House)

Museum of Photography – and Hafnarhús, part of the Reykjavík Art Museum.

Ljósmindasafn (Photography Museum)

MAP PAGE 34, POCKET MAP C3
Tryggvagata 15 ⓦ borgarsogusafn.is/ljosmyndasafn-reykjavikur. **Charge.**
The top floor of the city library building, **Grófarhús**, is given over to a changing exhibition of contemporary photography. Though the space is modest, **Ljósmindasafn** holds an impressive collection of around six million photographs, showcased alongside work from established visiting photographers. Moreover, the entire collection, which spans from 1870 to 2002, can now also be viewed online through the museum's website.

Hafnarhúsið (Harbour House)

MAP PAGE 34, POCKET MAP C3
Tryggvagata 17 ⓦ artmuseum.is. **Charge.**
The large, austere **Hafnarhúsið** was originally built in the 1930s as warehouse storage and office space for the Port of Reykjavík, but has now been converted into six large exhibition halls, connected by a corridor running above a central courtyard.

The museum plays host to frequently changing displays featuring contemporary Icelandic and international artwork, with one permanent exhibition dedicated to the multicoloured, cartoon-like work of Icelandic pop artist Erró.

There's certainly plenty of space here, but the overall layout is a little confusing, with an array of corridors – which once linked the former warehouse's storage areas – that twist and turn around the museum's supporting concrete and steel pillars.

Art for sale

With so much art on display in this relatively small city, it can be tempting to purchase an original Icelandic work while you're in Reykjavík. Should the urge strike, there are a couple of galleries worth checking out where you'll find a range of artists and styles represented: the long-established **i8** – outposts at Tryggvagata 18 (ⓦ i8.is; free) and at Marshall House (see page 42) – works with a group of around twenty artists, both Icelandic and international, who produce contemporary fine art; and **Hverfisgallerí**, just a few blocks away at Hverfisgata 4 (ⓦ hverfisgalleri.is; free), where sixteen of the seventeen artists represented are Icelandic, and the style is again contemporary fine art. Exhibitions at both galleries tend to run for around five weeks, though the newer i8 venue at Marshall House specializes in single-artist, long-form exhibitions.

The Viking

Shops

Fischersund
MAP PAGE 34, POCKET MAP C3
Fischersund 3 Ⓦ fischersund.com.
This family-run perfumery and art collective is the brainchild of self-taught nose Jónsi Birgisson – of Icelandic rock band Sigur Rós fame – and his three sisters, Inga, Lilja and Rosa. Perfumes are hand-crafted from Icelandic oils and herbs, with curious concoctions like bestseller No 23, designed to evoke smoke in the air, mowed grass, a beached whale and tobacco leaves with notes of black pepper and Icelandic Sitka spruce. A small museum traces the history of the island through scent.

Kolaportið
MAP PAGE 34, POCKET MAP D3
Tryggvagata 19 Ⓦ kolaportid.is.
Iceland's biggest flea market is housed in a cavernous building where you'll find any number of secondhand and new items. There's also a food section that, among other things, stocks unusual delicacies such as shark meat.

The Viking
MAP PAGE 34, POCKET MAP C3
Hafnarstræti 1–3 Ⓦ theviking.is.
From pens to fridge magnets, sheepskin rugs to woollen sweaters, this popular souvenir shop has got you covered. There's also a collection of books about Iceland, plus postcards.

Kolaportið

Restaurants

Bæjarins Beztu Pylsur

MAP PAGE 34, POCKET MAP D3

Tryggvagata 1 ⓦ bbp.is.

Hidden away on a patch of waste ground between Tryggvagata and Hafnarstræti, *Bæjarins* is a local institution, having opened in 1937. From a small and unassuming kiosk, it serves up the Nordic classic: a *pylsa* (hot dog) made with Icelandic lamb. Ask for *eina með öllu* – "one with everything" – for the whole shebang: the tasty sausage topped with a heap of fried onions, thick remoulade sauce and lashings of ketchup and mustard. Be prepared to queue; this haunt is extremely popular. Kr

BRÚT Restaurant

MAP PAGE 34, POCKET MAP D3

Pósthússtræti 2 ⓦ brut.is.

A seafood-leaning menu takes in the likes of marinated scallops and garlic-laced Icelandic whelks, though a smattering of meaty dishes (steak and chips) and vegetarian plates (watermelon

The iconic *Bæjarins Beztu Pylsur* hot dog

carpaccio, cauliflower 'steak') ensures no one feels left out. With a recommendation in the Michelin Guide, this is the place to go for fine wine and food pairings, served in a buzzy space. You will need deep pockets for this one, mind you. KrKrKrKr

Fish Market

MAP PAGE 34, POCKET MAP C4

Aðalstræti 12 ⓦ fiskmarkadurinn.is.

Smart, stylish restaurant, with wooden floors and clouds of fake greenery, attracting a lively after-work crowd. It specializes in Asian fusion dishes – try the grilled blue ling or the angelica-fed organic lamb. All produce is bought direct from Icelandic fishermen and farmers. KrKrKrKr

Grillhúsið

MAP PAGE 34, POCKET MAP C3

Tryggvagata 20 ⓦ grillhusid.is.

Popular and informal grill restaurant, particularly busy in the evening over weekends, decked out to resemble an American diner. The menu runs to pricey steaks, but it's best for its simple but delicious dishes like burgers and fish and chips. KrKr

Hornið

MAP PAGE 34, POCKET MAP D3

Hafnarstræti 15 ⓦ hornid.is.

Another classic Reykjavík restaurant that's stood the test of time – this one has been here since 1979 and is popular with locals for its excellent pizzas and pasta dishes. Also does a good range of meat and fish options, such as salted cod or slow-cooked lamb shank. KrKr

Reykjavík Fish Restaurant

MAP PAGE 34, POCKET MAP B2

Tryggvagata 8 ⓦ reykjavikfish.is.

Excellent restaurant showcasing the bounty of the sea in all manner of inventive guises, from *plokkari* (traditional fish stew) to garlic-drenched Arctic char and

Fish Market

a mixed seafood platter, plus the classic fish and chips. Also serves a tasty Icelandic meat soup and a selection of decent burgers (beef, fish, vegetarian and chicken). KrKr

Café

Kaffi Ó-le

MAP PAGE 34, POCKET MAP D3
Hafnarstræti 11 ⓦ facebook.com/KaffiOle.
This uber-cool speciality coffee shop is helmed by barista-owner Tom who knows how to whip up an excellent single-origin espresso. A small selection of freshly prepared sandwiches and home-made cakes is a tempting diversion. Kr

Bars

Dubliner

MAP PAGE 34, POCKET MAP C3
Naustin 1 ☏ 527 3232.
Iceland's first-ever Irish pub still draws in the crowds – and deservedly so. It's always a good choice for a convivial evening pint, and there's a reasonable selection of whiskeys, plus live music (often Irish folk and R&B) most nights of the week.

Frederiksen Ale House

MAP PAGE 34, POCKET MAP C3
Hafnarstræti 5
ⓦ facebook.com/frederiksenalehouse.
This well-located pub is busy at any time of day. There's a decent selection of draught and bottled beers, including Víking classic, Thule and stout. The expert staff are also adept at knocking up wicked cocktails. A fun spot for a night out.

Gaukurinn

MAP PAGE 34, POCKET MAP C3
Tryggvagata 22 ⓦ gaukurinn.is.
Long-established live-music venue and drinking den that's been drawing the crowds since even before beer was legalized in 1989. You'll find a mix of live music performances, karaoke sessions, open mic nights and pub quiz events (see the website for details).

The harbour

North of Geirsgata, the busy main road which runs parallel to the shoreline, lies Reykjavík harbour, built around reclaimed land – the beach where vessels once unloaded their foreign goods is now well inland from here. Street names in this area, such as Ægisgata (Ocean Street) and Öldugata (Wave Street), reflect the importance of the sea to the city, and a stroll along the dockside demonstrates Iceland's dependence on the Atlantic, with fishing trawlers being checked over and prepared for their next battle against the waves, and plastic crates of ice-packed cod awaiting transportation to village stores around the country. Keep an eye out, too, for the black whaling ships, each with a red "H" painted on its funnel (hvalur is Icelandic for "whale"), which are usually moored here. Ironically, the harbour is also the departure point for whale-watching and puffin-spotting tours.

Saga Museum

MAP PAGE 41, POCKET MAP A1
Grandagarður 2 ⓦ sagamuseum.is. Charge.
Housed in a former fish storehouse on the western edge of the harbour, the excellent **Saga Museum** is Iceland's answer to Madame Tussauds. The expertly crafted wax models of characters from the sagas and their reconstructed farms and homes are employed, superbly, to depict medieval Icelandic life,

often a misunderstood period in the country's history. A visit here will give you a sense of what life must have been like in Iceland centuries ago, and all the big names are here: poet and historian **Snorri Sturluson** (see page 94), who even breathes deeply as he ponders; Eirík the Red; and explorer Leifur Eiríksson (see page 60) and his sister Freyðis, the latter portrayed slicing off her breast as

Saga Museum

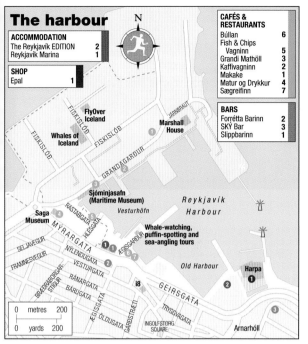

The harbour

ACCOMMODATION

The Reykjavik EDITION	2
Reykjavík Marina	1

SHOP

Epal	1

CAFÉS & RESTAURANTS

Búlan	6
Fish & Chips Vagninn	5
Grandi Mathöll	3
Kaffivagninn	2
Makake	1
Matur og Drykkur	4
Sægreifinn	7

BARS

Forrétta Barinn	2
SKÝ Bar	3
Slippbarinn	1

a solitary stand against the natives of Vínland who, after killing one of her compatriots, turned on her – according to the sagas, Freyðis's actions saw her aggressors immediately take flight. An informative audioguide (included in the admission fee) explains a little about each of the characters on display – and also about the smells of the period, which have been synthetically reproduced too.

Sjóminjasafn (Maritime Museum)

MAP PAGE 41, POCKET MAP M1

Grandagarður 8

Ⓦ maritimemuseum.is. Charge.

Given Iceland's prominence as a seafaring nation, Reykjavík's **Maritime Museum** is a big disappointment. A ragtag collection of old fishing hooks, dried fish and model boats, this tired exhibition of fisheries through the ages is dull in the extreme. The only saving

grace is the former coastguard vessel, *Óðinn*, moored in the dock outside (daily guided tours at 1pm, 2pm & 3pm). Built in Denmark in 1959, the ship patrolled Iceland's territorial waters in the North Atlantic until 2006, taking part in all three cod wars with the UK. The cutters used to slice through the nets of British trawlers are displayed on *Óðinn*'s rear deck.

Whales of Iceland

MAP PAGE 41, POCKET MAP M1

Fiskislóð 23 Ⓦ whalesoficeland.is. Charge.

This creative museum has drawn criticism over its entry fee, but it offers a unique opportunity (in Iceland) to appreciate the full magnificence of these massive mammals, whose true bulk is hidden beneath the surface of the water. Located in a vast purpose-built warehouse, the museum contains 23 life-size models suspended from the ceiling;

Whales of Iceland

walking among them gives an amazing perspective on their size. Exceptionally well executed, with steel skeletons and silicon skins, the models were made in China and shipped to Iceland in sections – the blue whale, for example, is as long as a tennis court. There are models of most species: the sperm whale, humpback, minke and even beluga.

FlyOver Iceland

MAP PAGE 41, POCKET MAP M1
Fiskislóð 43 Ⓦ flyovericeland.com. Charge.
Just next door to Whales of Iceland is **FlyOver Iceland**, an incredible

Harpa, a striking design by Olafur Eliasson

virtual-reality experience that involves being suspended in a moving seat while a VR headset transports you through Iceland's awe-inspiring mountains, glaciers and wildflower-choked meadows. While it obviously doesn't compare to the real deal, it's a fine back-up option for exploring the island's diverse landscapes, particularly if you're sticking to the city. Other exhibits include a Viking longhouse, while a short oversight of Iceland's culture and mythology is shared by the museum's resident troll.

Marshall House

MAP PAGE 41, POCKET MAP M1
Grandagarður 20
Ⓦ marshallhusid.is. Charge.
Marshall House is a multipurpose arts and cultural centre set in a former fish factory. It is home to a string of exhibition spaces, including the Living Art Museum; non-profit gallery Kling & Bang; and i8 Grandi, the gallery's second, larger outpost and host to single-artist, long-term exhibitions. The top floor shelters the studio of Icelandic-Danish artist Olafur Eliasson, famed for his large-scale, climate-centric installations – you might recognize him from *The Weather Project*, an immersive exhibition conjuring light and fog in Tate Modern's Turbine Hall, and the 139ft cascading

Waterfall in the grounds of the Palace of Versailles. The ground floor also houses the *Primavera* restaurant.

Harpa

MAP PAGE 41, POCKET MAP E2
Austurbakki 2 🌐 harpa.is. Free.
A striking addition to the Reykjavík skyline, **Harpa** is the brainchild of Ólafur Elíasson. The opera house's faceted facade is composed of hexagonal glass cubes, designed to resemble the basalt columns seen all over Iceland; during the winter, light shows illuminate the glass panels, producing dynamic displays of colour and shape. Inside, **Eldborg** is Iceland's premier venue for concerts and plays. Harpa is also home to the Icelandic symphony orchestra and national opera. Visitors are free to wander around the building at leisure, and the harbour-view café is a good people-watching spot.

Whale watching, puffin spotting and sea angling

Whale watching

Tours leave throughout the year (up to twelve departures daily depending on the season), sailing for Faxaflói bay north of Reykjavík. You're most likely to encounter minke whales, white-beaked dolphins and harbour porpoises, though orcas, humpbacks and dolphins can also be spotted; blue, fin and sei whales will also occasionally put in an appearance. You can check the success rate of sightings on previous trips on the company websites below, and should you fail to see any whales or dolphins on your tour, the companies will offer you a free trip, which can be taken at any time within the next two years.

Puffin spotting

Between mid-May and mid-August (after which the birds head out to sea for the winter months), there are twice-daily tours around the islands of Lundey and Akurey, where puffins gather to breed in the summer. Although it's not possible to go ashore, you'll have a great view of the cliffs and grassy slopes which make up the islands' sides, and the burrows where the puffins live. Remember, though, that puffin numbers have fallen in recent years due to a lack of the birds' main source of food, the sand eel. It's a good idea to ask about the tide conditions before choosing a departure because the boats get closer to the islands on a high tide.

Sea angling

Between May and August, sea-angling tours depart three times daily from the harbour, giving you a chance to try out your deep-sea skills – you get to keep anything you catch. Catfish, cod, haddock, mackerel and pollack are the most commonly landed, and you can barbecue your catch on board, should you choose.

Operators

Recommended operators include Elding on Ægisgarður (🌐 elding.is), which offers whale watching, puffin spotting and sea angling; and Special Tours, also on Ægisgarður (🌐 specialtours.is), which offers the same activities.

Shop

Epal

MAP PAGE 41, POCKET MAP E2
Inside Harpa concert hall, Austurbakki 2
ⓦ epal.is.
Showcase for Scandinavia's top design houses such as Normann Copenhagen, Design House Stockholm, Marimekko and Iittala.

Restaurants

Búllan

MAP PAGE 41, POCKET MAP B2
Geirsgata 1 ⓦ bullan.is.
This unimpressive little 1950s concrete bunker of a building at the harbour feels like an American diner inside – and it serves almost nothing but burgers and excellent fries. Expect to queue. Kr

Fish & Chips Vagninn

MAP PAGE 41, POCKET MAP B1
On the seafront at the junction of Rastargata and Hlésgata
ⓦ fishandchipsvagninn.is.
Owned by three Icelandic families who have all lived and worked in the UK in the seafood business, this mobile trailer serves deliciously fresh, British-style takeaway fish and chips – the fish is Icelandic, the chips are from Dutch potatoes, and the trailer is from Leeds in West Yorkshire. There is a handful of outside tables and chairs for alfresco eats. Kr

Grandi Mathöll

MAP PAGE 41, POCKET MAP M1
Grandagarður 16 ⓦ grandimatholl.is.
A warehouse-turned-food hall in the harbour, popular with a young local crowd. A scattering of vendors surrounds long wooden benches, offering everything from Vietnamese spring rolls to Korean barbecue, plus, of course, fresh fish and seafood – usually with an Asian fusion twist. Kr

Kaffivagninn

MAP PAGE 41, POCKET MAP M1
Grandagarður 10 ⓦ kaffivagninn.is.
Claiming to be the oldest eating establishment in Reykjavík, this fishermen's café down in the harbour is great for breakfast (served till 11am), fish-centric lunches/early dinners (11am–9pm) or weekend brunches. Also

Matur og Drykkur

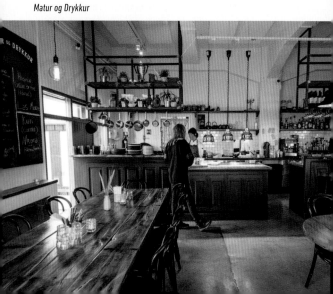

specializes in Danish-style open sandwiches as well as serving a wide range of cakes. KrKr

Makake

MAP PAGE 41, POCKET MAP C2
Grandagarður 101 Ⓦ makake.is.
A former sailors' canteen has been reimagined as a cool dim sum and ramen joint, with old beer crates standing in as tables, and lights made from repurposed Bundaberg ginger-beer bottles. Its dumplings are the culinary star of the show, though the small plates are just as tasty – think braised daikon drizzled with red-miso butter sauce. KrKr

Matur og Drykkur

MAP PAGE 41, POCKET MAP A1
Grandagarður 2 Ⓦ maturogdrykkur.is.
This inventive restaurant, plainly decked out with a concrete floor and wooden tables, has a truly unusual menu, featuring items such as an entire baked cod's head, with throat muscles in batter on the side. Offers only an evening six-course set menu (14,900kr). KrKrKrKr

Sægreifinn

MAP PAGE 41, POCKET MAP B2
Geirsgata 8
Ⓦ facebook.com/saegreifinn.seabaron.
This harbourside fishmonger-restaurant might look unimpressive from the outside –just a pale green weatherboard shack – but it's a favourite haunt of in-the-know locals after the best lobster soup in town. There's plenty of seasonal fresh fish on the menu, too, such as halibut, served on skewers. KrKr

Bars

Forrétta Barinn

MAP PAGE 41, POCKET MAP B2
Nýlendugata 14 Ⓦ forrettabarinn.is.
This funky bar-restaurant serves a good range of beers from Icelandic brewery Kaldi, as well

Sægreifinn

as international brands like Stella, Hoegaarden, Pilsner Urquell and Leffe. During happy hour (daily 4–6pm), you can get a beer here from 850kr.

SKÝ Bar

MAP PAGE 41, POCKET MAP F3
Inside Centerhotel Arnarhvoll, Ingólfsstræti 1 Ⓦ skyreykjavik.com.
Sip a cocktail at this sleek rooftop bar – part of the *Centerhotel* – while enjoying superb views out towards the opera house and on a clear day all the way to Mount Esja. It runs a daily extended happy hour (4–8pm) and rustles up well-prepared canapés and a few more substantial bar snacks, such as BLT and club sandwiches.

Slippbarinn

MAP PAGE 41, POCKET MAP B1
Mýrargata 2–8 Ⓦ slippbarinn.is.
This swanky and sophisticated place, inside the *Icelandair Reykjavík Marina* hotel (see page 113), has to be the most novel location for a bar in the whole of town – right beside the slipway where the ships come in to be repainted and repaired.

Tjörnin and around

From the harbour, Pósthússtræti leads south past the bars and restaurants of Tryggvagata, Hafnarstræti and Austurstræti to Tjörnin, which is invariably translated into English as "the lake" or "the pond". Tjörn and its genitive form of tjarnar are actually old Viking words, still used in northern English dialects as "tarn" to denote a mountain lake. Originally a lagoon inside the reef that once occupied the spot where Hafnarstræti now runs, this sizeable body of water, roughly a couple of square kilometres in size, is populated by forty to fifty varieties of birds – including the notorious arctic tern, known for their dive-bombing attacks on passers-by, which are found at the lake's quieter southern end. The precise numbers of the lake's bird population are charted on noticeboards stationed at several points along the bank.

Ráðhúsið (City Hall)

MAP PAGE 47, POCKET MAP C5
Tjarnargata 11. Free.

Occupying prime position on the northern edge of Tjörnin is **Ráðhúsið**. Opened in 1992, it's a showpiece of Nordic design, a modernist rectangular structure of steel, glass and chrome that actually sits on the lake itself. Inside, in addition to the city's administration offices, is a small café and, in one of the small exhibition areas, a fabulous self-standing **topographical model** of Iceland that gives an excellent impression of the country's unforgiving geography – you can marvel at the

Ráðhúsið (City Hall)

Tjörnin and around

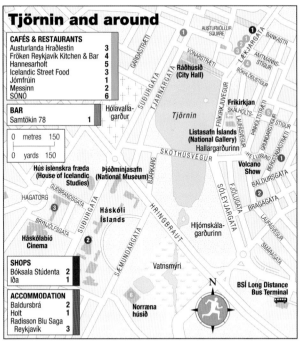

CAFÉS & RESTAURANTS	
Austurlanda Hraðlestin	3
Fröken Reykjavík Kitchen & Bar	4
Hannesarholt	5
Icelandic Street Food	3
Jómfrúin	1
Messinn	2
SÓNÓ	6

BAR	
Samtökin 78	1

SHOPS	
Bóksala Stúdenta	2
Iða	1

ACCOMMODATION	
Baldursbrá	2
Holt	1
Radisson Blu Saga Reykjavík	3

sheer size of the Vatnajökull glacier in the southeast (as big as the English county of Yorkshire) and the table mountains of the West Fjords, and gain instant respect for the people who live amid such challenging landscapes.

Suðurgata

MAP PAGE 47, POCKET MAP B5

One of the best views of Reykjavík can be had from **Suðurgata**, a street running parallel to Tjörnin's western shore; to get there from the City Hall, walk west along Vonarstræti, crossing Tjarnargata. Suðurgata is lined with tidy little dwellings, but from it you can see across the lake to the city centre's suburban houses, whose corrugated-iron roofs, ranging in colour from a pallid two-tone green to bright blues and reds, have been carefully maintained by their owners – the familiar picture-postcard view of Reykjavík.

Þjóðminjasafn (National Museum)

MAP PAGE 47, POCKET MAP A7

Suðurgata 41 ⊕ thjodminjasafn.is. Charge.

By far the most engaging part of the **Þjóðminjasafn** is the **first floor**, which covers the period from 800 to 1600; the video presentation within the "Origin of Icelanders" exhibition, devoted to the early Viking period and the use of DNA testing, is particularly good. Recent genetic research has shown that whereas around eighty percent of today's Icelanders are of Nordic origin, sixty-two percent of the early Viking-era women originated from the British Isles; the conclusion reached is that the first settlers sailed from Scandinavia to Iceland, stopping off at the British Isles along the way to marry.

Another prime exhibit is the small human figure, about the size of a thumb and made of bronze, which is thought to be over a

Statue overlooking Tjörnin

in Fljótsdalur, dating from around 1200, and depicting the medieval tale *Le Chevalier au Lion*: it features an ancient warrior on horseback slugging it out with an unruly dragon. The Danish authorities finally gave up the treasure in 1930 and returned the door to Iceland, together with a host of medieval manuscripts. Check out, too, the impressive Romanesque-style carved Madonna dating from around 1200, which hails from northern Iceland and is displayed within the "Medieval church" section.

The **second floor** of the museum, devoted to the period from 1600 onwards, canters through key events in Icelandic history such as the Trade Monopoly (1602–1787) and the birth of the republic. The displays conclude with a revolving airport-style conveyor belt laden with twentieth-century appliances and knick-knacks, featuring everything from a Björk LP to a milking machine.

thousand years old and to portray either the Norse god Þór or Christ. More spectacular is the carved church door from Valþjófsstaður

Magnússon's manuscripts

Despite so many of Iceland's sagas and histories being written down by medieval monks for purposes of posterity, there existed no suitable means of protecting them from the country's damp climate, and within a few centuries these unique artefacts were rotting away. Enter **Árni Magnússon** (1663–1730), humanist, antiquarian and professor at the University of Copenhagen, who attempted to ensure the preservation of as many of the manuscripts as possible by sending them to Denmark for safekeeping. Although he completed his task in 1720, eight years later many of them went up in flames in the Great Fire of Copenhagen, and Árni died a heartbroken man fifteen months later, never having accepted his failure to rescue the manuscripts, despite braving the flames himself.

In 1961, legislation was passed in Denmark decreeing that manuscripts composed or translated by Icelanders should be returned, but it took a further ruling by the Danish Supreme Court, in March 1971, to get things moving. Finally, however, in April of that year, a Danish naval frigate carried the first texts, Konungsbók Eddukvæða and Flateyjarbók, across the Atlantic into Reykjavík, to be met by crowds bearing signs reading "handritin heim" ("the manuscripts are home") and waving Icelandic flags. The new **Hús íslenskra fræða** (House of Icelandic Studies), finally completed in 2023, is set to house the collection.

All aboard!

Next stop, Reykjavík Central Station... As curious as it sounds in a country prone to any number of earth tremors and eruptions, plans to build a **railway line** from central Reykjavík to Keflavík airport by 2024 are being seriously considered. Due to its inhospitable terrain and low population, Iceland is one of the few European countries not to have a rail network of any kind. However, if plans get the go-ahead, that will all change, with a high-speed track laid across the lavafields of the Reykjanes Peninsula, drastically reducing the journey time to the international airport and cutting exhaust emissions. Although no site has been officially earmarked for a train station in Reykjavík, the favourite remains the rather ramshackle BSÍ bus terminal, which could then be transformed into a modern transport interchange fit for a capital city. Currently, the bus station is owned by Reykjavík Excursions who operate the Flybus to Keflavík airport.

The House of Icelandic Studies

MAP PAGE 47, POCKET MAP A7
Arngrímsgata.

Opposite the National Museum, the long-awaited **House of Icelandic Studies** (Hús íslenskra fræða) was finally completed in 2023. Dedicated to the preservation of Icelandic language and cultural heritage, the new centre is set to house the Árni Magnússon Institute's collection of medieval manuscripts (see box, page 48). A collection of the sagas and histories will be on display in an exhibition hall, while other rooms will be given over to research and conservation of the precious documents. Part of the University of Iceland, the large oval metal-clad and glass building has been named Edda, a nod to seminal work in the study of old Norse poetry.

Listasafn Íslands (National Gallery)

MAP PAGE 47, POCKET MAP D6
Fríkirkjuvegur 7 ⊛ listasafn.is. Charge.

A few minutes' walk north from the National Museum down Sóleyjargata, which runs along the eastern side of Tjörnin, passing the offices of the Icelandic president at the corner of Skothúsvegur, is the **Fríkirkjan** (Free Lutheran Church). The best feature of this simple wooden structure, painted whitish grey, is its high green roof and tall tower, useful as a landmark to guide you to the neighbouring former ice house, known as **Herðubreið**. Once a storage place for massive chunks of ice, hewn in winter from the frozen lake and used to preserve fish stocks, the building has been enlarged and completely redesigned, and houses **Listasafn Íslands** (the National Gallery of Iceland). Icelandic art may lack worldwide recognition, but all the significant names are to be found here, including Erró, Jón Stefánsson, Ásgrímur Jónsson, Guðmundur Þorsteinsson and Einar Hákonarson – though, disappointingly, lack of space (there are only three small exhibition rooms containing barely twenty or so paintings each) means that the works can only be shown in strictly rationed portions from the museum's enormous stock of around eleven thousand pieces of art. You can get an idea of the paintings not on display by glancing through the postcards sold at reception.

Shops

Bóksala Stúdenta

MAP PAGE 47, POCKET MAP M3
Sæmundurgata 4 Ⓦ boksala.is.
This bookshop, which belongs to the university, is probably the best-stocked in Iceland. It holds a wide range of teach-yourself-Icelandic texts, as well as glossy coffee-table books about the country.

Iða

MAP PAGE 47, POCKET MAP D4
Lækjargata 2a Ⓦ ida.is.
Engaging gift store selling a range of tasteful souvenirs from Iceland. Also doubles as a mini-bookshop, with a selection of travel guides and other books about the country.

Cafés and restaurants

Austurlanda Hraðlestin

MAP PAGE 47, POCKET MAP D4
Lækjargata 8 Ⓦ hradlestin.is.
Sporting the most un-Icelandic name you could imagine, "Oriental Express Train" boasts that its menu is full of genuine Indian dishes, though its offerings are tempered to the more conservative Icelandic palate. Kr

Fröken Reykjavík Kitchen & Bar

MAP PAGE 47, POCKET MAP D5
Lækjargata 24 Ⓦ frokenrvk.is.
At this chic restaurant, local ingredients are whipped into inventive dishes like lamb tartare with artichoke or salt-baked celeriac with creamy mushrooms and angelica. Don't miss the brambleberry sorbet with Omnom chocolate mousse. The brunch buffet (Sat & Sun 11am–2pm) at 6900Kr per person is a fun affair. The table to book is in the cosy winter garden room, or grab a front-row seat to the culinary theatre of the open kitchen in the Art Deco-styled dining room. KrKrKrKr

Hannesarholt

MAP PAGE 47, POCKET MAP E6
Grundarstigur 10 Ⓣ 511 1904.
Former home of Iceland's first prime minister, Hannes Hafstein,

Bóksala Stúdenta

now a beautifully restored café-restaurant. The menu is fairly limited, but excellent cakes and coffee aside, there's usually fish of the day, vegetarian pie and a toe-warming traditional stew on offer. Weekend events range from music concerts to Icelandic folk sing-alongs. KrKr

Icelandic Street Food

MAP PAGE 47, POCKET MAP D4
Lækjargata 8 ⓦ icelandicfoods.com.
Dinky family-run restaurant serving up a small selection of Icelandic eats at affordable prices. Recipes are passed down through the generations from grandma, who also rustles together sweet treats like pancakes and happy marriage cake. Savoury standouts include the lamb stew (with free refills until you're full, or the bread bowl collapses in on itself) and shellfish soup. Free waffles, too. Kr

Jómfrúin

MAP PAGE 47, POCKET MAP D4
Lækjargata 4 ⓦ jomfruin.is.
Jómfrúin is a popular Danish-influenced place specializing in *smørrebrød* (open rye sandwiches). All you have to do is pick your toppings: smoked salmon, caviar, asparagus, smoked eel or scrambled egg, perhaps. Fried plaice is the house speciality. KrKr

Messinn

MAP PAGE 47, POCKET MAP D4
Lækjargata 6 ⓦ messinn.com.
Seafood restaurant specializing in fish pans: *plokkfiskur*, cod, ling, wolffish, Arctic char, salmon – all cooked to perfection. Order the lobster soup to start, it's delicious. Friendly staff and buzzy vibe. Best to reserve in advance; it's popular. KrKrKr

SÓNÓ

MAP PAGE 47, POCKET MAP M3
Sturlugata 5 ⓦ sonomatseljur.is.
Located in the Nordic House cultural centre, this new, uber-

Messinn

chic restaurant has a regularly changing, season-driven vegan and vegetarian menu, usually featuring soup, a salad, pasta and open sandwiches. Dishes are made with fresh vegetables from its own kitchen-garden and flavoured with Icelandic foraged herbs. Also a good spot for a relaxed coffee, perfect for washing down one of its home-made cakes or melt-in-the-mouth pastries. Kr

Bar

Samtökin 78

MAP PAGE 47, POCKET MAP C4
Suðurgata 3 ⓦ samtokin78.is.
Once a week, Reykjavík's gay community gathers here at the premises of the Icelandic national LGBTQ+ association, Samtökin '78, for a relaxed evening of chat, discussion and the chance to socialize over a beer or a coffee. Also hosts the occasional event; check the website for upcoming dates. The community centre is also open to non-Icelanders, and you can always be assured of a warm and friendly welcome.

Bankastræti and around

Northeast of the National Gallery, Lækjartorg Square is bounded to the east by Bankastræti and by Lækjargata to the south. Lækjargata once marked the eastern boundary of the town and Tjörnin still empties into the sea through a small brook which now runs under the road here (lækjar comes from lækur, meaning "brook") – occasionally, when there's an exceptionally high tide, seawater gushes back along the brook, pouring into Tjörnin. The cluster of old timber buildings up on the small hill immediately south of Bankastræti is known as Bernhöftsstofan and, following extensive renovation, it now houses a couple of chichi fish restaurants (see page 57). Named after Tönnies Daniel Bernhöft, a Dane who ran a nearby bakery, it's flanked to the north by one of Iceland's most important buildings, Stjórnarráðshúsið.

Menntaskólinn and Stjórnarráðshúsið

MAP PAGE 54, POCKET MAP D4–D5
Both closed to the public.

Reykjavík's elegant old Grammar School, **Menntaskólinn**, built in 1844, once had to be accessed by a bridge over the brook. It also housed the Alþingi before the completion of the current Alþingishúsið (see page 28) in nearby Austurvöllur Square. Just north of Bankastræti, the small, unobtrusive white building at the foot of Arnahóll hill (see page 53) is, in fact, one of

Menntaskólinn

the seats of power in Iceland: **Stjórnarráðshúsið** (Government House) contains the cramped working quarters of the prime minister. It's one of the city's oldest-surviving buildings, built in 1761–71 as a prison.

Arnahóll

MAP PAGE 54, POCKET MAP E3

Up on **Arnahóll**, the grassy mound behind the Icelandic prime minister's offices, a statue of Ingólfur Arnarson, Reykjavík's first settler, surveys his domain; with his back turned on the National Theatre, and the government ministries to his right, he looks out to the ocean that brought him here over eleven centuries ago.

Experts believe this is the most likely spot where the pillars of Ingólfur's high seat – a sort of Viking-era throne – finally washed up; according to *Landnámabók*, they were found "by Arnarhváll below the heath".

Hverfisgata

MAP PAGE 54, POCKET MAP E4–K6

One of central Reykjavík's main thoroughfares, **Hverfisgata** has always played second fiddle to its more glitzy neighbour to the south, Laugavegur. True, it has fewer bars, restaurants and shops than Laugavegur, but a recent makeover has improved things greatly – new pavements have been laid and the whole street has been spruced up. Hverfisgata is at its grandest at its southern end – it's here you'll find the elegant **Danish Embassy** at no. 29 and also the former National Library, now the Safnahús museum, just a few doors down.

Safnahús (Culture House)

MAP PAGE 54, POCKET MAP E4

Hverfisgata 15 🌐 culturehouse.is. Charge. Sadly, the **Safnahús** has lost its way. Once the home of a remarkable exhibition about Iceland's medieval manuscripts (see box, page 48), today the

Arnahóll

museum has been subject to an amateurish makeover and contains nothing more than a hotchpotch of seemingly random items from the country's past. While individual pieces may impress, the overriding impression left on the visitor by the muddled exhibition (known as "Points of View") is one of disappointment – this could, and should, be so much better.

Though the **ground floor** is predominantly given over to a collection of religious art, it also, confusingly, contains more contemporary items such as a photographic portrait of former Icelandic president, Vigdís Finnbogadóttir, plonked alongside an ornate seventeenth-century tapestry and a sculpture of Mary from the church in Vatnsfjörður, dated around 1400–1500. It's a juxtaposition which doesn't work. Elsewhere on the ground floor, however, do look out for the various versions of *Jónsbók*, a grouping of ancient legal texts which date from 1281; most impressive is the modern copy of a text from 1363, replete with ornately decorated initial letters.

Bankastræti and around

SHOPS

12 Tónar	5
66° North	1
Aurum	2
Dogma	4
Handprjónasamband Íslands	6
Stefánsbúð	3

The **first and second floors** contain a mishmash of exhibits – and, once again, the ad hoc combination of items is quite arbitrary: for example, a magnificent altar piece from the church at Grenjaðarstaður, dating from 1766, rubs shoulders with a garish piece of modern art from 1948, *Big sister and little brother*

Laugavegur, or "washing road", the former route of washerwomen to Laugardalur springs

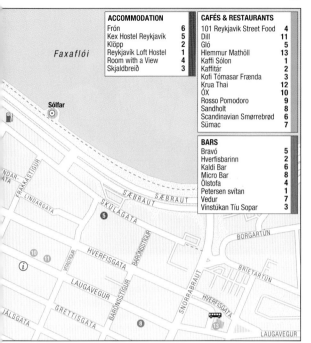

ACCOMMODATION	
Frón	6
Kex Hostel Reykjavík	5
Klöpp	2
Reykjavík Loft Hostel	1
Room with a View	4
Skjaldbreið	3

CAFÉS & RESTAURANTS	
101 Reykjavik Street Food	4
Dill	11
Gló	5
Hlemmur Mathöll	13
Kaffi Sólon	1
Kaffitár	2
Kofi Tómasar Frænda	3
Krua Thai	12
ÖX	10
Rosso Pomodoro	9
Sandholt	8
Scandinavian Smørrebrød	6
Sümac	7

BARS	
Bravó	5
Hverfisbarinn	2
Kaldi Bar	6
Micro Bar	8
Ölstofa	4
Petersen svitan	1
Vedur	7
Vínstúkan Tíu Sopar	3

by Kristján Davíðsson. That said, it's worth seeking out the stuffed **great auk**, hidden away in a small alcove off the main staircase leading to the top floor. Bought at auction in London in 1971, it's thought the bird was killed at Hólmsberg on the Reykjanes Peninsula (see page 80) – the last two great auks in the world were bludgeoned to death on June 3, 1844 on the nearby island of Eldey.

Laugavegur

MAP PAGE 54, POCKET MAP G5–K6

From Lækjartorg, turn right into the short Bankastræti and on, up the small hill, into **Laugavegur** (either "washing road" or "hot spring road"), the route once taken by local washerwomen to the springs in Laugardalur. This is Iceland's major commercial artery, and although it has lost some local business in recent years to nearby shopping malls, it has survived by going upmarket or niche – you'll find many of the stylish domestic outdoor gear stores here, alongside a smattering of arty design shops. There's also a fair number of cafés, bars and restaurants, not to mention the infamous Icelandic Phallological Museum (see page 61), given away by the tourist hordes milling outside. Not surprisingly, therefore, on Friday and Saturday evenings in summer it's bumper to bumper with cars, horns blaring and with well-oiled revellers hanging out of the passenger windows. However, during the summer months, large sections of Laugavegur are accessible only to pedestrians and cyclists – a decision by the City Council that has been warmly welcomed by the majority of the city's population, who have long complained that this was one of the city's worst bottlenecks.

Handprjónsamband Íslands

Shops

12 Tónar

MAP PAGE 54, POCKET MAP F5
Skólavörðustígur 15
Ⓦ 12tonar.company.site.
Cool record store and indie music
label, offering vinyl, coffee, live
gigs, specialist literature and comfy
sofas to enjoy it all from.

66° North

MAP PAGE 54, POCKET MAP E4
Bankastræti 5 Ⓦ 66north.com.
Renowned for good-quality
(if expensive) clothes that are
guaranteed to keep the worst of the
Icelandic weather at bay – there's
more than a grain of truth in its
slogan: "Keeping Iceland warm
since 1926".

Aurum

MAP PAGE 54, POCKET MAP E4
Bankastræti 4 Ⓦ aurum.is.
Contemporary Nordic design: one
half of the store features very cool
jewellery in silver, lava and gold;
the other side is full of quirky art
pieces for the home. Anyone for a
raven hanging mobile?

Dogma

MAP PAGE 54, POCKET MAP G5
Laugavegur 32
Ⓦ facebook.com/dogmaiceland.
If you're after a T-shirt as a souvenir
of your stay in Reykjavík, chances
are you'll find a strong contender
here. It stocks the classic *ég tala ekki
íslensku* ("I don't speak Icelandic")
range, among others.

Handprjónasamband
Íslands

MAP PAGE 54, POCKET MAP F5
Skólavörðustígur 19 Ⓦ handknit.is.
The Icelandic Handknitting
Association sells an astounding
number of home-made woollens.
Each item has been produced by a
knitter in the Reykjavík area, and
quality is high – and so are prices.
Tax-free shopping available (see
page 129).

Stefánsbúð

MAP PAGE 54, POCKET MAP E4
Laugavegur 7 Ⓦ stefansbud.com.
Designer Stefán Svan Aðalheiðarson
has teamed up with concept store
P3 to create Reykjavik's most-loved
vintage store – where he repairs
and sells preloved designer items

on the behalf of their owners. The curated collection of high-end and independent brands is packed with rare finds like 1990s Gucci.

Cafés and Restaurants

101 Reykjavik Street Food

MAP PAGE 54, POCKET MAP E5
Skólavörðustígur 8
Ⓦ 101reykjavikstreetfood.is.
Behind its canary-yellow facade, this unassuming restaurant dishes up a menu of classic Icelandic dishes such as lamb soup and fish stew. The fish and chips is a perennial favourite. KrKr

Dill

MAP PAGE 54, POCKET MAP H5
Laugavegur 59 Ⓦ dillrestaurant.is.
The first restaurant to hold a Michelin star in Iceland, *Dill* helped to raise the culinary bar in Reykjavík. Drawing on the natural larder of the island, the menu is packed with inventive field-to-fork dishes. No vegan options. KrKrKrKr

Gló

Kaffi Sólon

Gló

MAP PAGE 54, POCKET MAP F5
Laugavegur 20B Ⓦ glo.is.
This bright, airy and very popular vegetarian place serves up an array of fresh, healthy salads and warm comforting dishes along the lines of parsley root soup with hummus or nut stew. The emphasis is very much on farm-to-table produce, with much of it served uncooked. Also sells a wide range of just-squeezed juices. Kr

Hlemmur Mathöll

MAP PAGE 54, POCKET MAP K6
Laugavegur 20B Ⓦ hlemmurmatholl.is.
The old bus terminal has been repurposed as a food hall. Vendors include artisan bakery *Brauð & Co*, *Jómfrúin* of smørrebrød fame, Mexican taco haunt *La Poblana*, and *Skál!*, which gives a contemporary twist to Icelandic fare. Don't miss the *banh mi* from the Vietnamese food truck. KrKr

Kaffi Sólon

MAP PAGE 54, POCKET MAP E4
Bankastræti 7a Ⓦ solon.is/en.
Decked out in contemporary Icelandic design, this is one of

Vietnamese street food at Hlemmur Mathöll

Reykjavík's most popular cafés and serves a good range of meals – from vegan burgers and baked Arctic char to steaks and schnitzels. KrKr

Kaffitár
MAP PAGE 54, POCKET MAP E4
Bankastræti 8 Ⓦ kaffitar.is.
The Icelandic version of Starbucks, but with far better coffee, made from expertly blended beans. The usual run of cakes and muffins too, plus good croissants. Kr

Kofi Tómasar Frænda
MAP PAGE 54, POCKET MAP E4
Laugavegur 2 ☏ 551 1855.
Trendy young Reykjavíkers flock to this chilled place, also known simply as *Kofinn*, to loll around on the comfy couches, chat, drink coffee and work on their poetry. Its prime spot on Laugavegur is great for people-watching.

Krua Thai
MAP PAGE 54, POCKET MAP F6
Skólavörðustíg 21a Ⓦ kruathai.is.
This cosy, no-nonsense Thai place offers exceptional value, with a huge choice of single-dish meals – green curry, pad thai and

the like. Servings are generous. At lunchtime, a portion of three different set dishes with rice goes for a mere 2050kr. Kr

ÓX
MAP PAGE 54, POCKET MAP H6
Laugavegur 55 Ⓦ ox.restaurant.
The intimate 16-seat *Óx* is the second restaurant in Iceland to scoop a Michelin star. Chef Þráinn Freyr Vigfússon conjures up twelve courses of playful dishes that showcase the island's natural larder. It's like a fun dinner party: all guests start their tasting menu at the same time, feasting on sharing platters like saddle of lamb flavoured with native herbs. Reservation only. KrKrKrKr

Rosso Pomodoro
MAP PAGE 54, POCKET MAP G5
Laugavegur 40 Ⓦ rossopomodoro.is.
A genuinely good southern Italian restaurant, drawing inspiration from Neapolitan cuisine. Expect the usual: pizzas, pasta, salads and mains like grilled chicken with Parma ham, mozzarella and red wine sauce. KrKr

Sandholt

MAP PAGE 54, POCKET MAP G5
Laugavegur 36 ⓦ sandholt.is.
The best café-bakery in town
with good coffee and excellent
strawberry tarts, cinnamon
swirls, flans, fresh sandwiches
and handmade chocolates. Also
serves breakfast, including fresh
croissants, muesli and *skyr*. Kr

Scandinavian Smørrebrød

MAP PAGE 54, POCKET MAP F5
Laugavegur 22A ⓦ scandinavian.is.
Despite the name, this place
serves mainly Icelandic rather
than Scandinavian specialities,
such as reindeer pâté, lobster
soup and lamb dishes. KrKrKr

Sümac

MAP PAGE 54, POCKET MAP G5
Laugavegur 28 ⓦ sumac.is.
The brainchild of Þráinn Freyr
Vigfússon – of *ÓX* fame (see page
58) – *Sümac* has been turning
heads on the restaurant scene
since opening in 2017. Icelandic
ingredients are given a Lebanese/
Moroccan spin here; think deep-
fried cod cheeks with sumac-spiked
aioli or cured salmon served with
candied kumquats. KrKrKr

Bars

Bravó

MAP PAGE 54, POCKET MAP F5
Laugavegur 22 ☎ 823 7892.
In various guises, this spot has been
one of Reykjavík's most popular
bars for years, and is a great place
to start the evening. The music is
varied, encompassing everything
from electro to indie and pop.

Hverfisbarinn

MAP PAGE 54, POCKET MAP F4
Hverfisgata 20.
Hverfisbarinn is now back in
business after a makeover and
still attracts a young, cool
crowd. There are often long
queues to get in.

Kaldi Bar

MAP PAGE 54, POCKET MAP F5
Laugavegur 20B ⓦ kaldibar.com.
Kaldi Bar serves up any number of
beers from the Kaldi microbrewery
in Árskógssandur, near Akureyri.
It plays low music, so it's a sound
place to chat over a drink. It's
usually packed, though.

Micro Bar

MAP PAGE 54, POCKET MAP J6
Laugavegur 86 ⓦ gaedingur.beer/en/
pages/microbar-reykjavik.
Micro Bar serves eighty or so
different craft beers from around
the world, plus a range produced
by Iceland's microbreweries.

Ölstofa

MAP PAGE 54, POCKET MAP F5
Vegamótastígur 101.
Local drinking den with an
excellent selection of beer; be sure
to try a pint of Brió, the pub's
award-winning house brew.

Petersen svítan

MAP PAGE 54, POCKET MAP E4
Ingólfsstræti 2a ⓦ gamlabio.is.
For a drink with a view, head to
this lively rooftop terrace bar,
sitting pretty on top of historic
cinema Gamla Bíó. Often hosts live
music and has a daily happy hour.

Vedur

MAP PAGE 54, POCKET MAP F5
Klapparstígur 33 ⓦ verdurbarinn.is.
Very relaxed place whose eccentric
Spanish manager mixes magnificent
cocktails and serves up free tapas
while you sit sipping at the bar.

Vínstúkan Tíu Sopar

MAP PAGE 54, POCKET MAP F5
Laugavegur 27 ⓦ natturuvin.is.
One for the serious oenophiles,
this chic Nordic-style bar is filled
to the rafters with natural, organic
wines, many from small makers.
Nibble on small plates of cured
cod with black-garlic mayonnaise
or tindur, a local cheese served
with brown butter and hazelnuts.

Hallgrímskirkja and around

From the western end of Laugavegur, Skólavörðustígur streaks steeply upwards to the largest church in the country, the magnificent Hallgrímskirkja, a magnet for all tourists visiting Reykjavík. With its burgeoning number of shops and restaurants, the street is fast becoming a rival to Laugavegur, albeit in shorter form. Thanks to its hilltop vantage point, meanwhile, the church enjoys some of the best views of central Reykjavík of anywhere in the city. From Hallgrímskirkja, it's an easy stroll back down the hill, perhaps detouring via the excellent swimming pool, Sundhöllin (see page 124), towards Hlemmur, Reykjavík's main bus interchange, and on to the seafront. Here, there are sweeping views out over Faxaflói bay across to Mount Esja in the distance.

Hallgrímskirkja

MAP PAGE 62, POCKET MAP G7
Skólavörðuholt ⓦ hallgrimskirkja.is. Free; viewing platform charge.

The Reykjavík skyline is dominated by this modern concrete structure, with its neatly composed, space-shuttle-like form. Work began on the church – named after the renowned seventeenth-century

Hallgrímskirkja

religious poet Hallgrímur Pétursson – immediately after World War II, but was only completed in 1986, the slow progress due to the task being carried out by a family firm comprising one man and his son. The work of state architect Guðjón Samúelsson, the church's unusual design – not least its 73m-high steeple – has divided the city over the years, although locals have grown to accept rather than love it since its consecration.

Most people rave about the **pipe organ** inside, the only decoration in an otherwise completely bare, Gothic-style shell; measuring a whopping 15m in height and possessing over five thousand pipes, it really has to be heard (during services) to be believed. The tower has a **viewing platform**, accessed by a lift from just within the main door, giving stunning panoramic views across Reykjavík; note that it's open to the elements.

Leifur Eiríksson statue

MAP PAGE 62, POCKET MAP G7
With his back to the church and his gaze firmly planted on Vínland, the imposing statue of **Leifur Eiríksson**, the Icelandic explorer

Time is of the essence

Spend any time in Reykjavík and you'll soon understand that the city lives at the mercy of the elements. Rain and snow storms can appear as if from nowhere and howling winds, tearing straight in off the sea, can cut through all but the most robust of outdoor gear. Understand that and it's easy to see why no two public clocks in Reykjavík tell the same time. Exposure to the sea, altitude and general meteorological mayhem cause radically diverse wind conditions in different parts of the city. At the top of Hallgrímskirkja tower, for example, the wind is so strong that the hands on the clock are frequently blown off course. It's something Icelanders don't give a second thought to, of course, but it's not unusual to spot baffled tourists double-checking their watches to make sure of the correct time.

who is considered by many to have discovered North America, was donated by the US in 1930 to mark the Icelandic parliament's thousandth birthday.

This is one of the highest parts of Reykjavík, and on a clear day there are picturesque **views** out over the surrounding townhouses adorned with multicoloured corrugated-iron facades.

Einar Jónsson Museum

MAP PAGE 62, POCKET MAP F7
Eiríksgata 3 ⓦ lej.is. Charge.
The heroic form of Leifur Eiríksson is found in several other statues around the city, many of them the work of **Einar Jónsson** (1874–1954), who is remembered by this museum, housed in a pebble-dash building to the right of Hallgrímskirkja. Einar lived here in an increasingly reclusive manner until his death in 1954; a specially constructed group of rooms, connected by slim corridors and a spiral staircase, takes the visitor through a chronological survey of Einar's career. His style of sculpture varies widely, though is often influenced by his spiritual beliefs and by Icelandic mythology. If the museum is closed, peek into the **garden** at the rear, where there are several examples of Einar's work on display; his most visible work, the statue of independence leader Jón

Sigurðsson, stands in front of the Alþingishúsið (see page 28).

Phallological Museum

MAP PAGE 62, POCKET MAP K6
Laugavegur 116 ⓦ phallus.is. Charge.
The **Phallological Museum** is easy to spot – just look for the bemused-looking tourists standing outside, not quite believing that this is, indeed, a museum dedicated to the penis. Visitors can ogle the members of around three hundred mammals, displayed in jars of formaldehyde and alcohol. It's now possible to size up a human specimen too, following the death of 95-year-old Páll Arason, who had pledged his manhood to the museum (be warned – it comes complete with long white wisps of pubic hair).

And there's more: a misshapen foreskin removed in an emergency operation and a pair of human testicles are also on display. After that, you'll no doubt be ready for the plaster cast and photos of several former museum visitors, which leave very little to the imagination (you've been warned).

Sólfar

MAP PAGE 62, POCKET MAP H4
Sæbraut.
Down on Sæbraut, the main road which runs along Reykjavík's shoreline, sits the strikingly modern-

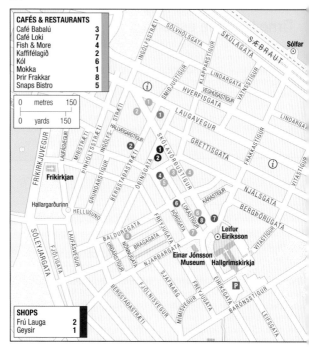

CAFÉS & RESTAURANTS	
Café Babalú	3
Café Loki	7
Fish & More	4
Kaffifélagið	2
Kól	6
Mokka	1
Þrir Frakkar	8
Snaps Bistro	5

SHOPS	
Frú Lauga	2
Geysir	1

looking sculpture **Sólfar** ("Sun Voyager"). Designed in shiny steel by the artist Jón Gunnar Árnason (1931–89), it depicts a stylized Viking longship, complete with crew and oars, sailing out north across the bay towards distant mountains – though Árnason himself stated that it was intended to depict a dream vessel floating off to new beginnings,

and wanted it to face westwards, towards the setting sun. Either way, it's an elegant – and much-photographed – piece.

Höfði

MAP PAGE 62, POCKET MAP P2
Borgartún. Closed to the public.
East of Sólfar, it's a five-minute stroll back along Sæbraut to **Höfði**,

Sólfar, a sculpture depicting a Viking longship

Hallgrímskirkja and around

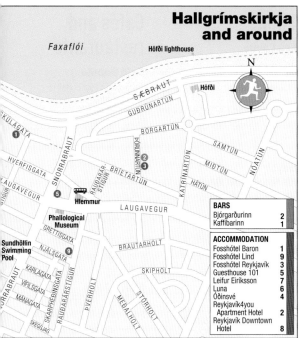

Faxaflói

Höfði lighthouse

BARS

Björgarðurinn	2
Kaffibarinn	1

ACCOMMODATION

Fosshótel Baron	1
Fosshótel Lind	9
Fosshótel Reykjavík	3
Guesthouse 101	5
Leifur Eiriksson	7
Luna	6
Óðinsvé	4
Reykjavik4you Apartment Hotel	2
Reykjavik Downtown Hotel	8

a stocky white wooden structure built in 1909 in Jungendstil, which occupies a grassy square beside the shore, between Sæbraut and Borgartún. Originally home to the French consul, the house also played host to Winston Churchill in 1941 when he visited British forces stationed in Iceland. Although Höfði is best known as the location for the 1986 snap summit between Soviet President Mikhail Gorbachev and US President Ronald Reagan, Icelanders know it equally well for its resident ghost, said to be that of a young girl who poisoned herself after being found guilty of incest with her brother.

Höfði lighthouse

MAP PAGE 62, POCKET MAP P2
Höfði House. Closed to the public.
Built in 2019, the canary-yellow Höfði lighthouse is a shiny new addition to Iceland's long maritime legacy. From 1945 to 2000, a tower at Sjómannaskólinn (Seaman's School) guided ships safely along the shore, until a cluster of high-rises blocked the light. The $1million lighthouse is based on traditional designs of the 1910s and has a viewing platform overlooking Faxaflói Bay and Mount Esja.

The 1909-built Höfði has a storied past

Shops

Frú Lauga
MAP PAGE 62, POCKET MAP F5
Óðinsgata 1 Ⓦ frulauga.is.
Farmers' market selling the
freshest of Icelandic fruit and
vegetables – from raspberries to
broccoli – delivered directly to
the shop every day from across
the country.

Geysir
MAP PAGE 62, POCKET MAP F5
Skólavörðustígur 16 Ⓦ geysir.com.
This is the only place you should
consider buying a pure wool
Icelandic blanket – even though
you'll need to part with around
30,000kr. The quality is far
superior to other shops, and tax-
free shopping is available.

Geysir

Cafés and restaurants

Café Babalú
MAP PAGE 62, POCKET MAP F6
Skólavörðustígur 22a Ⓦ babalu.is.
This quirky café occupies two
floors of a brightly painted
yellow building and is popular
with a bohemian crowd. Its
cheesecake is heavenly. Kr

Café Loki
MAP PAGE 62, POCKET MAP F7
Lokastígur 28 Ⓦ loki.is.
Traditional Icelandic food at good
prices: meat soup, herring plate,
sheep head jelly on flatbread and
skyr. Great views of Hallgrímskirkja
from upstairs. KrKrKr

Fish & More
MAP PAGE 62, POCKET MAP F6
Skólavörðustígur 23 Ⓦ salkakitchen.com.
Instead of battering and frying,
this fish restaurant steams the
catch; check the blackboard
to see what's fresh in that day.
There's often a deliciously tangy
fish soup, too. KrKr

Kaffifélagið
MAP PAGE 62, POCKET MAP E5
Skólavörðustígur 10 Ⓦ kaffifelagid.is.
Proudly boasting to be the
smallest café in the whole of
Iceland, this dinky spot serves
coffee produced by the Italian
company, Ottolina, which has
been in operation since 1947.
Ground coffee beans are also
available for purchase. Kr

Kól
MAP PAGE 62, POCKET MAP F6
Skólavörðustígur 40 Ⓦ kolrestaurant.is.
This classy place is named after
the *kól* (charcoal) over which the
meat is cooked: the grilled lamb
sirloin with polenta, carrots and
goat's cheese is delicious. The
fish – from charred salmon to
plaice – is also tasty. KrKrKrKr

Kaffifélagið, the smallest café in Iceland

Mokka

MAP PAGE 62, POCKET MAP E5
Skólavörðustígur 3a Ⓦ mokka.is.
Reykjavík's oldest café opened
in 1958, and was the first in
the country to serve espresso
and cappuccino to its curious
clientele. A changing display of
photographs adorns the walls,
and there's a no-music policy.

Þrir Frakkar

MAP PAGE 62, POCKET MAP E7
Baldursgata 14 Ⓦ 3frakkar.is.
A backstreet French-style bistro
with definite leanings towards
traditional Icelandic game: horse
tenderloin with mushrooms,
plokkfiskur (fish and potato mash)
and smoked guillemot. KrKr

Snaps Bistro

MAP PAGE 62, POCKET MAP F6
Þórsgata 1 Ⓦ snaps.is.
With wooden floors and swathes
of glass, this light-flooded bistro
is a chic spot for French cuisine
with an Icelandic twist. Excellent
wine list, too. KrKrKr

Bars

Bjórgarðurinn

MAP PAGE 62, POCKET MAP P2
Þórunnartún 1 Ⓦ bjorgardurinn.is.
Attached to the *Fosshótel*, the "Beer
Garden" has an impressive range
of beer both on tap and in bottles,
including pilsner, stout, pale ale
and brown ale. Happy hour is
4–7pm, when there are some great
deals to be had. Don't miss the
sausages in a brioche bun, either.

Kaffibarinn

MAP PAGE 62, POCKET MAP F5
Bergstaðastræti 1 Ⓦ kaffibarinn.is.
With an unmistakable red
corrugated-iron frontage
emblazoned with the famous
London underground logo, this
tiny bar fancies itself as an arty
hangout and trades on the rumour
that Blur's Damon Albarn owns it,
however unlikely. Be that as it may,
it's still perhaps your best bet for a
great night out in Reykjavík and is
a legend on the scene.

Öskjuhlíð and around

The wooded hill of Öskjuhlíð (60m above sea level) affords spectacular views of the city, and is a popular recreation area for Reykjavíkers, who flock here to explore the paths that crisscross its verdant slopes. Öskjuhlíð has, in fact, only been wooded since 1950, when a forestation programme began after soil erosion had left it barren and desolate. A plot of land on the hill's southern side, near the inlet of Fossvogur and the Fossvogskirkjugarður cemetery, has been earmarked as the location for a temple to the Æsir, the heathen gods of Viking times, though building work seems to have stalled for the time being.

Perlan

MAP PAGE 67, POCKET MAP N4
Öskjuhlíð ☎ 562 0200. Free.

If you arrive in Reykjavík from Keflavík airport, it's hard to miss the space-age-looking grey container tanks that sit at the top of the wooded hill, Öskjuhlíð. Each is capable of holding four thousand litres of water at 80°C for use in the capital's homes, offices and swimming pools; it's also from here that water has traditionally been

Perlan

pumped, via a network of specially constructed pipes, underneath Reykjavík's pavements to keep them ice- and snow-free during winter. **Perlan**'s name – The Pearl – comes from its glittering, glassy dome, which sits on top of the tanks and can be seen from miles away.

Being on top of a hill, the dome itself offers excellent 360-degree **panoramic views** of the entire city: simply take the lift to the fourth floor and step outside. On a clear day you can see all the way to the Snæfellsjökull glacier at the tip of the Snæfellsnes peninsula, as well as the entirety of Reykjavík. Before leaving, make sure you see the artificial indoor **geyser simulator** that erupts every few minutes from the basement, shooting a powerful jet of water all the way to the fourth floor: it's a good taste of what's to come if you're heading out to the real thing at Geysir (see page 89).

Nauthólsvík geothermal lagoon

MAP PAGE 67, POCKET MAP N4
Nauthólsvegur ⓦ nautholsvik.is. Charge.

At the southern end of Öskjuhlíð, close to the Reykjavík Sailing Club, there's an artificial beach of bright yellow sand, known as Ylströnd, where it's possible to swim in an enclosed **seawater lagoon** (the

Öskjuhlíð and around

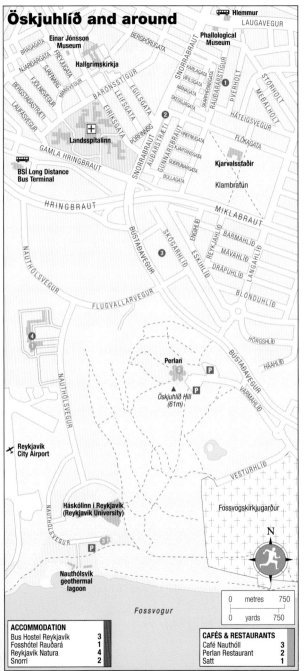

Einar Jónsson Museum

Hallgrímskirkja

Phallological Museum

Hlemmur

Landsspítalinn

BSÍ Long Distance Bus Terminal

Kjarvalsstaðir

Klambratún

Perlan

▲ Öskjuhlíð Hill (61m)

Reykjavik City Airport

Háskólinn í Reykjavík (Reykjavik University)

Fossvogskirkjugarður

Nauthólsvík geothermal lagoon

Fossvogur

N

metres	750
0	
yards	750
0	

ACCOMMODATION	
Bus Hostel Reykjavík	3
Fosshótel Rauðará	1
Reykjavik Natura	4
Snorri	2

CAFÉS & RESTAURANTS	
Café Nauthóll	3
Perlan Restaurant	2
Satt	1

water temperature is generally 15–19°C). There are also two hot pots located on the beach (around 38°C), one of which is built into the sand. In the winter, the temperature in the lagoon is a more invigorating 4–6°C.

Nauthólsvík is one of the best places in the city to relax and take the alfresco waters. Not only does the site offer great views of the southern coastline, but it's also unfenced and open to the surrounding countryside, meaning you can simply come and go as you please. Note that there are no lockers in the changing rooms themselves, just open baskets for your clothes, though it is possible to store valuables for 300kr – ask at the service centre. Remember, as at other Icelandic pools, you must thoroughly shower naked, without a swimming costume, before entering the hot pots.

Kjarvalsstaðir

MAP PAGE 67, POCKET MAP N3

Flókagata 24 ⓦ artmuseum.is. Charge.

The **Kjarvalsstaðir** art gallery is set in a 1970s Nordic Modernist building designed by Hannes Kr. Davíðsson: a squat edifice with concrete walls and swathes of glass arranged around a central courtyard. Though its exterior might be harsh, the interior is surprisingly bright and airy. Full-

length windows frame views of birch trees and grassy expanses, while a series of geometric skylights fills the space with natural light.

Part of the Reykjavík Art Museum, Kjarvalsstaðir is devoted to the work of Iceland's most celebrated artist, Jóhannes Sveinsson Kjarval (1885–1972). After working on a fishing trawler during his youth, Jóhannes moved abroad to study art, spending time in London, Copenhagen, France and Italy, but it was only after his return to Iceland in 1940 that he travelled widely in his own country, drawing on the raw beauty he saw around him for the quasi-abstract depictions of Icelandic landscapes which made him one of the country's most popular twentieth-century painters. Painted in oils, much of his work is a surreal fusion of colour: his bizarre yet pleasing *Krítik* ("Critique") from 1946–47, a melee of icy blues, whites and greys measuring a whopping 4m in length and 2m in height, is the centrepiece of the exhibition, portraying a naked man jauntily bending over to expose his testicles while catching a fish, watched over, rather oddly, by Norse warriors.

The museum is divided into two gallery halls – the east one shows Jóhannes's work, while the west hall is dedicated to touring temporary exhibitions.

Nauthólsvík geothermal lagoon

Kjarvalsstaðir art gallery

Cafés and restaurants

Café Nauthóll

MAP PAGE 67, POCKET MAP N4
Nauthólsvegur 106 Ⓦ nautholl.is.
This classy, airy bistro has large
windows overlooking Fossvogur
bay and serves a good selection
of tapas-style nibbles during the
day and more substantial mains
after 5pm. Also does a tempting
weekend brunch (3150kr).
KrKrKrKr

Perlan Restaurant

MAP PAGE 67, POCKET MAP N4
Varmahlíð 1 Ⓦ perlan.is.
A huge glass dome curves over
this light-flooded restaurant
on the fifth floor of Perlan,
offering views across the city and
mountains. Chefs Friðgeir Ingi
and Guðmundur rustle together
a menu of simple but satisfying
dishes like open sandwiches,
soups, salads and main meals
such as fish and chips. Next
door, the café offers cakes,
sandwiches and light bites. KrKr

Satt

MAP PAGE 67, POCKET MAP N3
Icelandair Hótel Natura, Nauthólsvegur 52
Ⓦ sattrestaurant.com.
Satt at *Icelandair Natura* offers a
value weekday lunch buffet and
a weekend brunch deal. The rest
of the menu is steep, but you're
paying for the setting. KrKrKr

Café Nauthóll

Eastern Reykjavík

After rambling through central Reykjavík for a good couple of kilometres, Laugavegur comes to an end at the junction with the main north–south artery, Kringlumýrarbraut. Beyond here, Suðurlandsbraut marks the southern reaches of Laugardalur valley, hemmed in between the low hills of Grensás to the south and the northerly Laugarás, just behind Sundahöfn harbour, whose Þvottalaugarnar springs have been known since the time of the Settlement as a source of hot water for washing. The springs are still here, the spot commemorated by the Ásmundur Sveinsson statue, Þvottakonan (The Washerwoman), while the area is also home to Iceland's premier sports ground; an indoor sporting and concert venue; the HI youth hostel and campsite; and the country's largest swimming pool.

Laugardalsvöllur and Laugardalshöll

MAP PAGE 72, POCKET MAP Q2

Open-air **Laugardalsvöllur** is the country's main sports stadium, hosting all of Iceland's international football and athletics fixtures. The largest attendance here was in 2004 for a friendly football match between Iceland and Italy, when over twenty thousand people packed into the ground to see the game – a staggering seven percent of the entire Icelandic population. Just to the south, across Engjavegur, **Laugardalshöll** hosts international indoor sporting events such as handball, volleyball and basketball. It is also the country's biggest concert venue, holding up to eleven thousand people. Should Iceland ever manage to win the Eurovision Song Contest (the dream of all Icelanders), Laugardalshöll would

Swimming etiquette in Iceland

One of the best things about a trip to Reykjavík is the chance to swim outdoors in the city's geothermally heated swimming pools, whose water usually hovers around 23–25°C, and to loll in divinely warm **hot pots**, which tend to vary between 35 and 39°C. Since water in both the pools and the hot pots doesn't contain chlorine, strict rules are in place to ensure that bathers do not contaminate the water. Firstly, you must leave your outdoor shoes on the racks provided at the entrance to the changing room. Then, having undressed, you must **shower naked**, without a swimming costume, washing your body thoroughly with the soap provided in the areas marked on the multilingual signs posted up in the shower rooms: feet, hair, underarms, groin and bottom. Duty attendants will not hesitate to berate you should they spot you breaking the rules. Squeaky clean, you can now enjoy Iceland's best natural resource.

Laugardalslaug, a Reykjavík institution

be the most likely choice of venue; Iceland came second in both 1999 and 2009.

Laugardalslaug

MAP PAGE 72, POCKET MAP Q2
Sundlaugavegur
Ⓦ reykjavik.is/laugardalslaug. Charge.
Since opening in 1968, the swimming complex **Laugardals-laug** has become a Reykjavík institution. It is the biggest in Iceland and features a 50m outdoor pool, a smaller children's pool and paddling pool, two waterslides, numerous hot pots, a steam sauna, gym and mini-golf.

Ásmundarsafn

MAP PAGE 72, POCKET MAP Q2
Sigtún Ⓦ artmuseum.is. Charge.
If sculpture is your thing, you'll want to check out the domed **Ásmundursafn**, dedicated to the work of **Ásmundur Sveinsson** and part of the Reykjavík Art Museum. Sveinsson (1893–1982) was one of the pioneers of Icelandic sculpture, and his powerful, often provocative, work was inspired by his country's nature and literature.

During the 1920s he studied in both Stockholm and Paris, returning to Iceland to develop his unique **sculptural Cubism**, a style infused with Icelandic myth and legend. You can view his work here at his former home, which he designed and built with his own hands between 1942 and 1950; he lived where the museum shop and reception are currently located.

The building is an uncommon shape for Reykjavík because, when Ásmundur planned it, he was experimenting with Mediterranean and North African themes, drawing particular inspiration from the domed houses common to Greece. The crescent-shaped building beyond the reception area contains examples of the sculptor's work, including several busts from his period of Greek influence. Note that the original of his most famous sculpture – 1926's **Sæmundur á selnum** (*Sæmundur on the Seal*), which shows one of the first Icelanders to receive a university education, the priest and historian Sæmundur Sigfússon (1056–1133), sitting astride a seal,

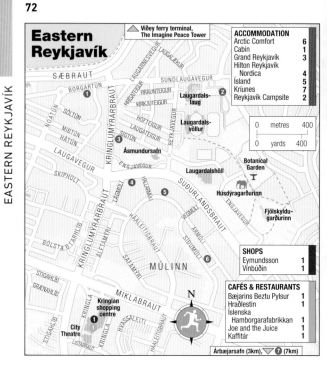

Eastern Reykjavík

△ Viðey ferry terminal, The Imagine Peace Tower

ACCOMMODATION

Arctic Comfort	6
Cabin	1
Grand Reykjavík	3
Hilton Reykjavík Nordica	4
Ísland	5
Kriunes	7
Reykjavik Campsite	2

SÆBRAUT
BORGARTÚN
NÓATÚN
SÖLTÚN
MIÐTÚN
HÁTÚN
LAUGAVEGUR
SKIPHOLT
KRINGLUMÝRARBRAUT
SIGTÚN
ENGJAVEGUR
LAUGATEIGUR
HOFTEIGUR
KIRKJUTEIGUR
HRAUNTEIGUR
HÁTEIGUR
LAUGARNESVEGUR
LAUGALÆKUR
SUNDLAUGAVEGUR
Laugardals- laug
Laugardals- völlur
Ásmundarsafn
Laugardalshöll
REYKJAVEGUR
HÁALEITISBRAUT
LÁGMÚLI
HALLARMÚLI
SUÐURLANDSBRAUT
VEGMÚLI
ÁRMÚLI
SÍÐUMÚLI
ENGJAVEGUR
Botanical Garden
Húsdýragarðurinn
Fjölskyldu- garðurinn
BÓLSTAÐARHLÍÐ
STIGAHLÍÐ
GRÆNAHLÍÐ
STIGAHLÍÐ
KRINGLUMÝRARBRAUT
ÁLFTAMÝRI
SAFAMÝRI
HÁALEITISBRAUT
MÚLINN
MIKLABRAUT
KRINGLA
Kringlan shopping centre
City Theatre
HVASSALEITI
HÁALEITISBRAUT
LISTABRAUT

N

0 metres 400

0 yards 400

SHOPS

Eymundsson	1
Vínbúðin	1

CAFÉS & RESTAURANTS

Bæjarins Beztu Pylsur	1
Hraðlestin	1
Íslenska Hamborgarafabrikkan	1
Joe and the Juice	1
Kaffitár	1

Árbæjarsafn (3km), ▽ 7 (7km)

psalter in hand – is not on display here; it stands outside the main university building on Suðurgata. You will, however, find a smaller version of the original in the museum grounds, where there are also lots of Ásmundur's other soft-edged, gently curved monuments

Reykjavík's lush Botanical Garden

to the ordinary working people of the country.

Botanical Garden

MAP PAGE 72, POCKET MAP Q3
Ⓦ facebook.com/grasagardur. Free.

The green expanses beyond the sports ground (Laugardalshöll) contain the country's most impressive **Botanical Garden**. Barely ten minutes on foot from the Ásmundur Sveinsson sculpture museum, reached by walking east along Engjavegur, the lush grounds contain an extensive collection of native Icelandic flora, as well as thousands of imported plants and trees. This place is particularly popular with Icelandic families, who come here not only to enjoy the surroundings but also for the adjoining family park and small zoo, which are a hit with children.

Húsdýragarðurinn and Fjölskyldugarðurinn

MAP PAGE 72, POCKET MAP Q3
Hafrafell Ⓦ mu.is. Charge. Buses #2, #15 and #17 run from the city centre; get off at the Laugardalshöll stop.

Especially with curious children in tow, **Husdýragarðurinn zoo** – home to Icelandic mammals such as seals, foxes, mink and reindeer, plus a handful of farm animals – makes for a thoroughly pleasant afternoon's visit. There's also a collection of fish caught in local rivers and lakes, which will keep younger visitors entertained. Once the attraction of the animals starts to wane, you can check out the surrounding **Fjölskyldugarðurin family park**, where there's a small duck lake complete with replica Viking longboat, a go-kart track, and other fun-filled activities based loosely around a Viking theme, including a fort and an outlaw hideout.

Kringlan shopping centre

MAP PAGE 72, POCKET MAP P3
Kringlan 4–12 Ⓦ kringlan.is. A free shuttle bus operates here from the city centre;

Árbæjarsafn open-air museum

check the website where you'll find departure times. Alternatively, city buses #1, #3, #4 and #6 all come here.

The construction in 1987 of **Kringlan shopping centre** – the biggest in Reykjavík, with some 170 stores – took place amid concerns that it would lead to the closure of many shops in the city centre. Those fears turned out to be unfounded, as both Kringlan and the city centre have experienced an unprecedented boom in recent years, which shows no signs of ending. In addition to its many stores – which are expensive but eature well-known international names such as Diesel, Boss and Timberland as well as home-grown outlets – Kringlan also boasts a library, theatre, cinema and a branch of the state-owned alcohol monopoly, *vínbúðin*.

Árbæjarsafn

MAP PAGE 72, POCKET MAP T2
Kistuhylur 4 Ⓦ arbaejarsafn.is. Charge.

The **Árbæjarsafn** open-air museum is a collection of turf-roofed and corrugated-iron buildings on the site of an ancient

Viðey dates back to the time of the Settlement

farm that was first mentioned in the sagas around the mid-1400s. The buildings and their contents record the sweeping changes that occurred as Iceland's economy switched from farming to fishing – the arrival of the fishing trawler in the nineteenth century heralded the beginning of the Icelandic industrial revolution – and Reykjavík's rapid expansion. The pretty **turf church** here, dating from 1842, was carefully moved to its present location from Skagafjörður on the north coast in 1960. Next to it, the farmhouse is dominated by an Ásmundur Sveinsson sculpture, *Woman Churning Milk*, illustrating an all-but-lost way of life.

Viðey

MAP PAGE 72, POCKET MAP R1
ⓦ elding.is/videy.
Reached by a short ferry ride from Sundahöfn harbour east of the city centre, and actually the top of an extinct volcano measuring barely 1.7 square kilometres, the island of **Viðey**

has a rich heritage dating back to the time of the Settlement. You can see it from the mainland by taking a ten-minute walk north of the Laugardalur area along Dalbraut, which later mutates into Sundagarður. If you fancy a brisk stroll with serene views of the ocean and a bit of alfresco art thrown in, this is the place to come.

The Imagine Peace Tower

MAP PAGE 72, POCKET MAP R1
ⓦ imaginepeacetower.com.
To the left of the ferry landing on Viðey, in the opposite direction to the church, the unusual wishing-well structure you can see is the **Imagine Peace Tower**. Conceived in 2007 by Yoko Ono as a beacon to world peace and inscribed with the words "imagine peace" in 24 languages, the structure emits a powerful tower of light every night between October 9 (John Lennon's birthday) and December 8 (the anniversary of his death), illuminating the Reykjavík sky.

Shops

Eymundsson

MAP PAGE 72, POCKET MAP P3
Kringlan shopping centre
Ⓦ eymundsson.is.
With a good selection of souvenirs,
presents, maps and magazines, as
well as coffee-table books about
Iceland, Eymundsson is always
worth a browse.

Vínbúðin

MAP PAGE 72, POCKET MAP P3
Kringlan shopping centre Ⓦ vinbudin.is.
Perfectly located for nipping in
to buy a bottle of wine while
out shopping at the Kringlan
centre, this outlet of *vínbúðin* is
one of the busiest in the country.
Knowledgeable staff are on hand
to offer advice if you're looking
for a specific tipple to match
a meal.

Cafés and restaurants

Bæjarins Beztu Pylsur

MAP PAGE 72, POCKET MAP P3
Kringlan shopping centre Ⓦ bbp.is.
If you're in the market for a quick
dine and dash, this long-standing
favourite will hit the spot. *Bæjarins*
claims that the combination it
offers of hot dogs with a remoulade
sauce is Iceland's national dish. Kr

Hraðlestin

MAP PAGE 72, POCKET MAP P3
Kringlan shopping centre
Ⓦ hradlestin.is.
Serving a range of Indian food
– including an Indian vegetarian
pizza – this is the place to come if
you've tired of Iceland's ubiquitous
fish of the day and lamb chops. The
carrot soup with ginger is good –
though remember that the dishes
are geared towards the conservative
Icelandic palate. KrKr

Íslenska Hamborgarafabrikkan

MAP PAGE 72, POCKET MAP P3
Kringlan shopping centre
Ⓦ fabrikkan.is.
This popular restaurant has a
huge choice of burgers, both
beef (cooked medium rare)
and chicken. Try the delicious
"Morthens", with bacon,
mushrooms, garlic and Béarnaise
sauce. Kr

Joe and the Juice

MAP PAGE 72, POCKET MAP P3
Kringlan shopping centre
Ⓦ joeandthejuice.is.
This enterprising juice bar and
café blitzes just about everything –
from avocado to ginger – into all
manner of delicious and healthy
concoctions. Kr

Kaffitár

MAP PAGE 72, POCKET MAP P3
Kringlan shopping centre Ⓦ kaffitar.is.
This chain opened in Kringlan in
1994 and is one of Reykjavíkers'
favourite coffeehouses. Grab a
panini, salad or home-made cake
from the café's own bakery –
perfect for taking a break from the
shopping marathon. Kr

Bæjarins Beztu Pylsur

EASTERN REYKJAVÍK

Hafnarfjörður and around

Set amid an extensive lavafield, Hafnarfjörður, just 10km southwest of the capital, is as big as the centre of Reykjavík, although much more provincial in flavour. It's worth making the 25-minute bus ride out here to sample some real Viking food at the town's Viking village, Fjörukráin, and to learn more about the Icelanders' obsession with elves, dwarves and other spiritual beings – Hafnarfjörður is renowned across Iceland as having the country's greatest concentration of huldufólk ("hidden people"). Another standout attraction worth heading out of Reykjavík for is the Sky Lagoon in Kópavogur, which opened in 2021 and is a quieter, but just as memorable, alternative to the tourist-choked Blue Lagoon further south.

Hafnarfjörður museum

MAP PAGE 77, POCKET MAP T2
Vesturgata 8. Free.

A stone's throw from the north end of Strandgata, a block north of the harbour, is **Hafnarfjörður museum**, housed in a wooden warehouse dating from the late 1800s and also known as Pakkhúsið. Inside is a passable if somewhat dull portrayal of Hafnarfjörður's life and times, featuring the likes of a stuffed goat and an old fishing boat.

Sívertsens-Hús

MAP PAGE 77, POCKET MAP T2
Vesturgata 6. Free.

Next door to Hafnarfjörður museum stands **Sívertsens-Hús**, the town's oldest building, dating from 1803 and once the residence of local trader, boat builder and man-about-town Bjarni Sívertsen. It's now home to a fairly interesting folk museum, stuffed to the gills with with how-we-used-to-live paraphernalia dating from the nineteenth century.

Hafnarfjörður harbour

Reykjavik (7km), Sky Lagoon (8km)

Hafnarfjörður and around

| 0 | metres | 200 |
| 0 | yards | 200 |

CAFÉS & RESTAURANTS

Fjaran	5
Fjörugarðurinn	6
Silfur	3
Súfistinn	1
Tilveran	2
Tuk Tuk Thai	4
Von	7

ACCOMMODATION

Hafnarfjörður Camping	2
Helguhús	3
Hótel Viking	4
Lava Hostel	1

Þríhnjúkahellir (22km)

Þríhnjúkahellir

MAP PAGE 77, POCKET MAP T2

Ⓦ insidethevolcano.com. Charge for tours, including return transport from Reykjavík.

About 20km southeast of Reykjavík, near the Bláfjöll ski area, lies **Þríhnjúkahellir**, an accessible, 4000-year-old subterranean **magma chamber** discovered in the 1970s which is like nowhere else in Iceland. There's little to see on the surface except for a small volcanic bump amid a landscape of moss and grass – but the scale below ground becomes clear once you've climbed into a **safety cage** and been lowered by crane into the 120m-deep space. Once you've touched down safely at the bottom, you're allowed to wander cautiously over the rough boulders and stones that carpet the floor of Þríhnjúkahellir's 30m-wide chamber.

Be sure to check out the walls, too, which are streaked in different colours left by molten minerals, all

twisted and spiked by the forces. Normally, a chamber such as this would fill with magma during an eruption and then solidify, but in Þríhnjúkahellir's case the molten rock drained out through tunnels, which are still visible at the sides of the cave floor.

Note that you should wear warm clothes and tough shoes or boots, as there is a 45-minute walk over rough ground at the beginning and end of the tour, to and from the volcano entrance. The tour ends with hot soup and bus transfer back to Reykjavík.

Sky Lagoon

MAP PAGE 77, POCKET MAP T2

Vesturvör 44–48 Ⓦ skylagoon.com. Charge. Kópavogur's big-hitting attraction is the **Sky Lagoon**, a geothermal spa that opened in 2021. Just a 15-minute drive from Reykjavík, the hot spring complex includes an infinity pool with views of

The hidden people

The street of Strandgata and neighbouring Austurgata in Hafnarfjörður are, according to Icelandic folklore, home to the town's population of **hidden people** – elves, dwarves and other spirits who live in entire families between the rocks that are dotted around the town centre. Apparently, elves are only visible to those with second sight, though a majority of Icelanders are quite prepared to admit they believe in them. In fact, an alarming number of new roads constructed across the country have been subject to minor detours around large rocks after workers attempted to move the boulders only to find that their diggers and earth movers broke down time and again in the process. Should you be keen to try out your second sight, occasional **tours** lasting a couple of hours leave from the tourist office at Laugavegur 5 (ⓦalfar.is); they weave their way through Hafnarfjörður, visiting the homes of the *huldufólk*, and are led by guide and storyteller Sigurbjörg Karlsdóttir.

the North Atlantic Ocean, an icy plunge pool, waterfall, cosy cavern bar, and a café set in a moss-cloaked, flint-walled building. The approach to the lagoon – past a soulless industrial estate – belies the sublime setting that awaits spa-goers: the pools are sculpted into cragged lava rocks along the wind-contoured coastline. Though most visitors make a beeline for the Blue Lagoon, this is a more affordable and just as memorable experience – without the crowds. Plus, it will be within walking distance once the long-planned foot, cycle and bus bridge is built. Visit at sunset for the finest light.

Hafnarfjörður is, according to Icelandic folklore, home to hidden people

Cafés and restaurants

Fjaran

MAP PAGE 77
Strandgata 55 Ⓦ fjorukrain.is.
This snug, wood-panelled restaurant in the Viking village is akin to a British country pub. It serves the same Viking delicacies as *Fjörugarðurinn*, but feels more refined (you'll get real plates rather than wooden platters). KrKrKrKr

Fjörugarðurinn

MAP PAGE 77
Strandgata 55 Ⓦ fjorukrain.is/restaurant.
Designed to resemble a Viking longhouse, this atmospheric place, decked out with candles and heavy wooden tables, serves a full Viking dinner of seafood soup, shark, dried haddock and lamb shank, all washed down with beer and Black Death schnapps, and ending on *skyr* for dessert. KrKrKr

Fjörugarðurinn

Silfur

MAP PAGE 77
Fjarðargata 13–15
Ⓦ silfur.wix.com/silfur.
This bright and airy café in the Fjörður mall enjoys views over the harbour and serves burgers, pasta, plus fish and chips. Kr

Súfistinn

MAP PAGE 77
Strandgata 9 Ⓦ sufistinn.is.
Hafnarfjörður's main coffeehouse, with outdoor seating for good weather. It's also a popular place for a beer of an evening. Kr

Tilveran

MAP PAGE 77
Linnetstígur 1 Ⓦ tilveranrestaurant.is.
A justifiably popular seafood restaurant, with daily lunch specials including soup, fish of the day and coffee; in the evening plump for a succulent fish dish or meaty options. KrKr

Tuk Tuk Thai

MAP PAGE 77
Fjarðargata 19 Ⓦ tuktukthai.is.
Pleasant restaurant serving well-priced one-dish Thai classics: think pad thai, green curry and massaman curry. Its takeaway packages are good value, too. KrKrKr

Von

MAP PAGE 77
Strandgata 75 Ⓦ vonmathus.is.
There's a Nordic feel to this smart but relaxed modern restaurant, with an emphasis on seasonal Icelandic ingredients. The menu is short, usually with a catch of the day and lamb. Perhaps better value are the set tasting menus (from 8500kr). KrKrKr

The Reykjanes Peninsula

Southwest of Reykjavík along the multi-lane Route 41, the Reykjanes Peninsula's rugged, lichen-covered lavafields jut out into the stormy waters of the Atlantic. Fagradalsfall, an active volcano in the centre of the peninsula, has been erupting on and off since 2021, with gushing lava occasionally visible from the capital. It would be hard to imagine a wilder place so close to the city, and yet here amid the seemingly bleak and lonely landscape are some real gems – not least the surreal splash of colour at the Blue Lagoon, Iceland's premier thermal spa. A couple of offbeat museums and a bizarre bridge in the middle of nowhere are worth a look in passing, but most of all it's the rocky, surf-streaked coastline, complete with associated birdlife, which rewards a day spent circuiting the peninsula: don't miss Selatangar's curious ruins, the great auk monument and seething mud pools at Reykjanestá, nor the teeming bird colonies at Hafnaberg and Krýsuvíkurberg. Key sights such as the Blue Lagoon are easily reached on buses, but elsewhere you'll need your own vehicle or to join a tour.

The Blue Lagoon

MAP PAGE 81, POCKET MAP S3
Off Route 43 near Grindavík, around 45km from Reykjavík Ⓦ bluelagoon.com. Charge; advance booking required.

The Blue Lagoon

Forget the crush of tour buses, or the extravagant entry fee: your first sight of the **Blue Lagoon**, with its steaming, milky blue waters pooling amid a wilderness of black

The Reykjanes Peninsula

Akranes

Hvalfjörður Tunnel

Grundarhvefi

Faxaflói

Mosfelsbær

REYKJAVIK

Garðskagi

Garður

Hafnarfjörður

Elliðavatn

Sandgerði

Keflavik International Airport

Keflavik

Þrihnjúka-hellir

Stafnes

Vikingheimar

Þríhnúkagígur

Njarðvík

Hafnir

Reykjanes Peninsula

REYKJANES-FÓLKVANGUR

Blue Lagoon

Kleifarvatn

Hliðarvatn

Hafnaberg Cliffs

Bridge Between Two Continents

Grindavik

Strandar-kirkja

Reykjanestá

Gunnhver Hot Springs

Kvikan Museum

Selatangar

Krýsuvíkurberg

ATLANTIC OCEAN

Eldey

miles 10
kilometres 15
N

ACCOMMODATION
Northern Light Inn 1
Strandarkirkja Campsite 2

CAFÉS & RESTAURANTS
Kaffi Duus 1
Lava Restaurant 2
Papa's 3
Pylsuvagninn 4

lava rubble, will make you glad you came to Iceland. Wade out into the shallow water (it's just about deep enough for swimming in places) or relax in the shallows, the heat seeping into your muscles; it's especially atmospheric on cold days, when a thick fog swirls and the waters feel even warmer.

The Blue Lagoon has its origins in local seawater, vaporized at the nearby **Svartsengi geothermal power station** and then fed – at a comfortable 38°C or so – into the lagoon. There's also a steam room, plus an artificial waterfall to stand under, while Icelanders scoop handfuls of silvery grey **silt** off the bottom of the lagoon to make facial mudpacks: it's said to cure skin disorders. Whatever the beneficial effects to your skin, your hair will take a real battering from the lagoon's mineral content; rub in plenty of conditioner as protection before bathing.

Vikingheimar (Viking World)

MAP PAGE 81, POCKET MAP S2
Víkingabraut 1, Njarðvík; heading west along Route 41, look for the cube-shaped building on the coast, about 5km before Keflavík town ⓦ vikingaheimar.is/en. Charge.

Despite their reputation as fearsome warriors, the Vikings were also great traders and travellers, and the centrepiece of **Vikingheimar** is the *Íslendingur*, a full-sized replica **Viking longship**. Before finding a home here, this working model crossed the Atlantic in 2000 to celebrate Leifur Eiríksson's discovery of "Vinland" (America), one thousand years earlier. The clinker-built wooden vessel is broad-beamed and must have been fairly stable, but it would still have taken some nerve to brave an Atlantic crossing without so much as a cabin to shelter under; you can walk around on deck, imagining

Lava tubes

Underneath the Reykjanes Peninsula's grey-green tumble of volcanic rubble is a complex network of **lava tubes**, many of which are unexplored. These tunnels were created when the sides of long, narrow lava flows cooled enough to harden and form an insulating tube around the molten centre, which continued to flow until the tunnel drained. Later eruptions buried the tubes, and they'd be unknown today if cave-ins hadn't revealed their presence. More are being discovered every year, but the current pick includes kilometre-long **Raufarhólshellir**, with its weird ice formations; the similarly scaled **Búri Cave**, only found in 2005; spectacular **Þríhnúkagígur** (though this is actually a drained magma chamber; see page 77); and **Leiðarendi**, which is perhaps the least exciting, but also the most accessible. Because of the dangers inherent in exploring the tubes, you should only visit them as part of a tour; try ⓦ extremeiceland.is or ⓦ insidethevolcano.com.

what being crammed alongside a bunch of seasick freebooters and their livestock must have been like.

Aside from the ship, the museum has an account of the brief Viking settlement of Vinland (poor rations and harsh weather eventually drove them back) and some period remains found locally, plus an engaging multimedia exhibition on Viking myths.

Hafnaberg Cliffs

MAP PAGE 81, POCKET MAP S3
West off Route 425, about 5km south of Hafnir village.

Iceland's old roadways were once marked by strings of large **stone cairns** known as "priests" (because, quip locals, they showed the path to salvation without ever taking it themselves). One such row survives on Reykjanes, with its tail-end marking a footpath leading 3km west from a roadside parking bay to the **Hafnaberg Cliffs**; along the way you need to watch out for overly protective greater skuas, which nest in the soft sand hereabouts. The cliffs themselves drop sheer into the sea, packed through the summer with thousands of nesting seabirds. Take care near the crumbly edges.

Bridge Between Two Continents

MAP PAGE 81, POCKET MAP S3
Beside Route 425, about 2km south from the Hafnaberg car park. Free.

The discrepancy between this structure's rather grand title and its appearance – an unimpressive metal footbridge crossing a small ravine – can't help but raise a smile. The gap that the **Bridge Between Two Continents** spans is supposedly part of the rift system where the North American and Eurasian continental plates are tearing apart. Nonetheless, it's all a bit ludicrous, and the "Welcome to America" and "Welcome to Europe" signs at either end – not to mention the monochrome gravel and black-sand scenery – add to the sense of fun.

Reykjanestá

MAP PAGE 81, POCKET MAP S3
Off Route 425 along a 2km-long good gravel road signposted "Reykjanesviti".

Reykjanestá is the Reykjanes Peninsula's southwestern extremity, a rocky, storm-battered headland whose geothermal potential is being tapped by **Reykjanesvirkjun**, the shiny 100MW power station that you pass on the way in. There's another thermal outlet nearby at **Gunnuhver hot springs**, a compact mess of boiling mud, hissing vents and clouds of sulphurous steam, which last blew itself apart in 2005 – check out the skeletons of boardwalks still dangling over the void. Traces of older building foundations can be seen and are evidence of former efforts to establish vegetable hothouses here.

Reykjanestá's main vehicle track ends at a coastal car park, where a tall white **lighthouse** stands slightly inland on a hillock; the original was sited on the grassy coastal headland opposite, but fell into the sea during an earthquake. A solidified lava flow from some ancient eruption forms a low platform above the waves; far out to sea you can just pick out the remote sea stack of **Eldey**, which hosts Europe's largest gannet colony. Eldey also has the sad distinction of being where the last known pair of great auks was bludgeoned to death in 1844; there's a giant **bronze auk** in the Reykjanestá car park as a memorial, its beak pointing seawards.

Kvikan Museum
MAP PAGE 81, POCKET MAP S3
Hafnargata 12a, Grindavík
Ⓦ grindavik.is/kvikan. Charge.
There are three separate exhibitions at **Kvikan**, but two – one on geothermal power, and another about local author and Spanish scholar Guðberg Bergsson – can safely be skipped in favour of **Saltfisksetur Íslands** (Icelandic Saltfish Museum). Even today, with tourism replacing fishing as Iceland's main source of income, the country owes a great deal to the cod: the national **coat of arms** was originally a golden cod, filleted and crowned on a red field, and the Icelandic Nobel Laureate, Halldor

Reykjanestá, the elemental southwestern tip of the Reykjanes Peninsula

Laxnes, wasn't exaggerating when he made the memorable comment, "*Lífið er saltfiskur*" ("life is saltfish"), back in the 1930s. Even so, a lack of timber for boatbuilding meant that Iceland only really became a fishing nation during the late nineteenth century, after the first modern vessels could be imported, but its success swiftly drew farmers off the land to settle in new coastal settlements around the country.

Today, saltfish still accounts for a good slice of Iceland's export earnings, with most of the product shipped to Spain and West Africa. The Saltfish Museum covers all this history brilliantly in models, dioramas, old photographs and – somehow – the authentic smell of salted cod.

Selatangar

MAP PAGE 81, POCKET MAP T3
12km east of Grindavík on Route 427, then south along short gravel road.
Selatangar was once an important seasonal fishing camp for southwestern Iceland, and though abandoned after better ports with modern vessels became established elsewhere during the nineteenth century, many of the settlement's **stone-block** structures survive among an eerie coastal landscape of grey sand and ancient, disintegrating lava flows. It's reached from the car park along a 200m-long path marked out with driftwood and other bits of flotsam, but you probably won't realize that you've arrived anywhere until you begin to notice small, roofless huts and walled-up recesses – careful investigation will uncover well over a dozen – all half-camouflaged among the volcanic boulders.

Selatangar must have been a tough place to live even in summer, given the pernicious fogs which keep materializing and dispersing along with the coastal breeze. Stories of hauntings by a lonely **ghost** named Tanga-Tómas add to the decidedly spooky atmosphere.

Krýsuvíkurberg

MAP PAGE 81, POCKET MAP T3
22km from Grindavík on Route 427, then turn south at a signpost marked "Krýsuvíkurbjarg" along a 4km gravel road. Be prepared to park the car and walk in if the road proves impassable.
On a sunny day, the seascapes from the top of **Krýsuvíkurberg** – a long, crescent-shaped bay of cliffs – are fabulous, the blue waters below contrasting with a clifftop layer of ochre soil and green grass. You might be lucky and see a couple of **puffins** here, but the main inhabitants at Krýsuvíkurberg are thousands of fulmars and kittiwakes, all of which you can hear long before you reach the top. The main headland is topped by a **triangulation point**, which makes a great spot to admire the scenery, from where you can follow the ridges inland and back around to the car park along unmarked tracks.

Strandarkirkja

MAP PAGE 81, POCKET MAP T3
Off the eastern end of Route 427, about 15km from Þorlákshöfn, via a short sealed road.
A neat, unassuming weatherboard church painted dove grey and black, offset by its warm and colourful interior, **Strandarkirkja** – the "**Church on the Seashore**" – was built around 1900 by grateful fishermen after they survived a shipwreck off the local coast. There was once a busy community here, but today only the church and a handful of scattered farm buildings remain; it's a beautiful spot, though, with green meadows protected from the seafront by a high stone wall. Walk along the shore and you'll probably see seals and plenty of eider ducks, but watch out if you try to stroll through the arctic tern colony along the approach road – they can turn nasty if you get too close.

Lava Restaurant at the Blue Lagoon

Cafés and restaurants

Kaffi Duus

MAP PAGE 81, POCKET MAP S2
Duusgata 10, Keflavík Ⓦ duus.is.
At first glance a straightforward place, but it's not just the tandoori chicken that has an Asian slant: Indian spices also seep into the bacon-wrapped monkfish and battered cod and chips. Pricey, but there are sea views and generous portions. KrKrKr

Lava Restaurant

MAP PAGE 81, POCKET MAP S3
Blue Lagoon Ⓦ bluelagoon.com.
Set right against a lava wall with views out over the lagoon, this place certainly enjoys a superb setting. The menu features "modern Icelandic" cuisine: the rack of lamb is excellent, as are the langoustine and fish of the day. Demands deep pockets. KrKrKrKr

Papa's

MAP PAGE 81, POCKET MAP S3
Opposite Kvikan museum at Hafnargata 7a, Grindavík Ⓦ papas.is.
Grillhouse serving good cod and chips, though its pizzas really steal the show: a "supreme" with everything is tempting, but best is the "TNT", loaded with pepperoni, black pepper, chillies and jalapeno sauce. Kr

Pylsuvagninn

MAP PAGE 81, POCKET MAP T3
Strandarkirkja, near the campsite Ⓦ pylsuvagninn.is.
This yellow mobile trailer sells canned drinks and, more importantly, *pylsur*: Icelandic hot dogs served with copious fried onions and remoulade sauce. There's an adjacent shelter shed with chairs and tables where you can eat if the weather's bad. Kr

Modern Icelandic food at *Lava Restaurant*

The Golden Circle

Spreading eastwards from Reykjavík, the route known as the Golden Circle ties together some of Iceland's most iconic landscapes and historic sights. The centrepiece is Þingvellir, a monumental rift valley where Iceland's original parliament met in Viking times, while the nearby cathedral at Skálholt once served as one of the country's two greatest religious pivots (along with Hólar in northern Iceland). Elsewhere, a web of roads weaves through the lush summertime landscape of meadows framed by distant snowcapped peaks, where you could spend a mellow half-day comparing the relative attractions of outdoor hot pools at Fontana Spa (luxurious) and the so-called "Secret Lagoon" (minimalist). Routes ultimately converge right on the edge of Iceland's barren wilds at Geysir, the original geyser after which all others are named, and the mighty waterfall of Gullfoss.

Þingvellir (Thingvellir) National Park

MAP PAGE 88, POCKET MAP U1
30km northeast of Reykjavík on Route 36
Ⓦ thingvellir.is/english.aspx. Free.
Þingvellir – the "Assembly Plains" – fill a 4km-wide, 40m-deep rift

valley that marks where the North American and Eurasian continental plates are tearing apart at the rate of 1.5cm every year. It was in this dramatic landscape that Iceland's entire population first gathered in the tenth century to hold an annual

Þingvellir National Park

The Alþing

From 960, Iceland's 36 regional chieftains convened the **Alþing**, or General Assembly, at Þingvellir (Thingvellir) for two weeks every summer. Almost the entire Icelandic population attended the event: tented camps were set up, people traded, gossiped, settled disputes at the four regional courts and listened to the **Lawspeaker** reciting the country's legal code. The highest penalty was being declared an "out-law" – banishment from Iceland for three years – yet, although the courts carried great authority, they had no concrete powers to enforce their decisions beyond making them public knowledge. If litigants felt themselves strong enough to ignore the courts they could do so, though at the risk that others would seek satisfaction privately. *Njál's Saga* (see box, page 96) contains a graphic account of such a battle between two feuding clans, which broke out at the Alþing itself in 1011 AD.

It was the Alþing's lack of real power that allowed Norway and then Denmark to take control of the country during the Middle Ages; by the late thirteenth century the lawspeaker's position was abolished and the courts stripped of all legislative authority. Though Iceland's Alþing survives to this day, restored with full powers after Independence from Denmark in 1944, the **last assembly** at Þingvellir was in 1798, after which the parliament relocated to Reykjavík.

assembly, thereby establishing a system of government which survived, in one form or another, for nearly a thousand years (see box, page 87).

Orientate yourself at the **viewpoint** next to the Visitor Centre on Route 36. South lies Iceland's largest lake, **Þingvallavatn**, from where the rift valley runs northeast for 16km, covered in a tangle of dwarf birch thickets and flanked by basalt columns, to Skjaldbreiður's distant, flattened cone – at 1060m, one of the highest peaks in view.

From the viewpoint, a footpath descends into the 2km-long **Almannagjá canyon** past Lögberg, the rock from where Iceland's laws were publicly recited in Viking times. Look out too for traces of *buðs*, roofed camps built as accommodation during assemblies. The path continues to where the narrow **Öxará** – the Axe River – splashes down into the rift over the western escarpment;

the rocks midstream are barely worn, supporting the story that the river was diverted during the tenth century to provide drinking water for the thirty thousand or so people who converged on Þingvellir each year. Under medieval Danish law, the site became an execution ground for witches and adulterers.

East over the river, Þingvellir's plain white **church** sits on a small rise, the only substantial building in the valley. The original structure was built in 1080 with support from the Norwegian king, though the present building dates from 1859. Two tombs out the back belong to the poets Einar Benediktsson and Jónas Hallgrímsson, both major forces in Iceland's nineteenth-century drive for political independence from Denmark; it's fitting that they were buried in a location so strongly tied to the national identity. While you're here, don't overlook **Flosagjá** and **Peningagjá**, deep volcanic fissures nearby, flooded by clear blue spring water.

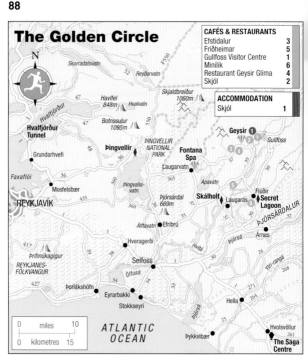

The Golden Circle

Fontana Spa

MAP PAGE 88, POCKET MAP V2
Hverabraut 1, Laugarvatn, 75km east of
Reykjavík; turn off Route 37 at the N1
roadhouse and follow the signs
ⓦ fontana.is. Charge.

This small open-air spa overlooks
the lakeshore at the tiny resort

Fontana Spa

town of **Laugarvatn** – which, in
typical Icelandic style, isn't much
more than a few houses. **Fontana**
itself sits literally on top of a
cauldron of bubbling hot springs,
which splutter and hiss noisily
below the sauna huts, pouring out
erratic clouds of steam.

There are also a couple of more
sedate tiled thermal pools; they're
very shallow, though – better
for sitting in with a beer ordered
from the bar (there's also a café
that serves light meals) than for
swimming. Visiting after dark
in winter is quite an experience,
especially when the Northern
Lights are putting on a show.

Skálholt

MAP PAGE 88, POCKET MAP U2
Off Route 35 on Route 31, 85km east of
Reykjavík ⓦ skalholt.is. Free.

The lush farming region above the
middle Hvítá – one of Iceland's
longest rivers – is known as the

"Bishop's Tongue". That might be because this is church land, overlooked from the top of a knoll by the historic **Skálholt cathedral**, which was founded as early as 1056 AD (Christianity had only been introduced in 1000 AD). The site went on to become a bustling centre of learning with a population in excess of two hundred people, making it the country's largest medieval settlement. The original wooden cathedral was eventually destroyed by an earthquake in the late eighteenth century, and the current cathedral – an unfussy black-and-white building – was only built and reconsecrated in 1963.

The **interior** is fairly sober too, with abstract stained-glass windows and a tapestry-like mosaic of Christ behind the altar providing the only colour. During the summer, the stone sarcophagus belonging to Bishop Páll Jónsson, a charismatic thirteenth-century churchman, is also on view to the public.

Outside, recent archeological excavations have exposed the foundations of the former bishop's residence. There's also a monument to Iceland's last Catholic bishop, Jón Arason, who was executed here during the religious wars of the sixteenth century.

Skálholt cathedral

Secret Lagoon

MAP PAGE 88, POCKET MAP V2
Off Route 30, at Hverahólmi, Flúðir, 100km east of Reykjavík; head north out of town and turn east immediately over the bridge ⓦ secretlagoon.is. Charge.

In contrast to the higher-profile Blue Lagoon and Fontana Spa, the "**Secret Lagoon**" is a low-tech affair – basically a large outdoor pond of gently steaming water. Purpose-built for recreation in the 1890s, it fell into disrepair after more modern swimming pools sprung up in neighbouring towns, and has only recently been renovated and reopened.

Geysir

MAP PAGE 88, POCKET MAP V1
Right beside Route 35, 100km east of Reykjavík. Free.

The **Geysir** thermal area occupies the edge of a grassy plain below

Touring the Golden Circle

Renting a car (see page 123) is the least expensive way for more than one person to cover the Golden Circle, even after factoring in fuel costs. Otherwise, the cheapest deal is on the daily Þingvellir–Laugarvatn–Geysir–Gullfoss **bus** run by Reykjavík Excursions (ⓦ re.is), which stops long enough at each place to have a brief look around. For a dedicated, nine-hour **Golden Circle Tour**, there's Reykjavík Excursions again, Gray Line (ⓦ grayline.is) and Sterna (ⓦ sternatravel.com), not to mention a host of smaller operators. It's best to book a day in advance in summer; all can collect from Reykjavík accommodation, and a guide provides commentary in English en route.

Bjaranarfell's 720m-high slopes, with steam from the dozen or so geysers here visible long before you arrive. The largest vent, **Geysir** itself, has been pretty much inactive for the last few decades. Instead, join the crowds surrounding **Strokkur**, "the Churn", which reliably fires its load 30m skywards every few minutes. Nobody is sure exactly what causes the eruptions, but watch closely and you'll see a dome of cooler water form on top of Strokkur's pool just before an eruption, which some experts believe acts as a "lid", allowing the pressure below to build up to bursting point. Take time to look at some of the smaller, less active vents, especially **Blesi**'s twin pools – one clear and colourless, the other opaque blue. There are no protective barriers at Geysir, in spite of the boiling hot pools; keep children supervised and under no circumstances put any part of your body in the springs.

Strokkur

Gullfoss

MAP PAGE 88, POCKET MAP V1
Route 35, about 107km east of Reykjavík.
Free.

Saved for the nation from being flooded by a hydro dam

Gullfoss

back in the 1920s, **Gullfoss** – the Golden Falls – forms a spectacular, thundering twin cataract across the Hvítá River: entering the mouth of a basalt gorge, the river drops 10m and then turns sharply, falling a further 20m into a sunless chasm from which spray fountains upwards in huge, soggy clouds, catching rainbows and giving the falls their name.

Adding to the spectacle is the location: look back the way you've come and all is green, but turn north and vistas take in a stark gravel plain spreading towards the distant mountain ridges and ice caps of Iceland's barren Interior (see page 104).

In winter, the canyon is covered in curtains of ice, and the waterfalls, brought nearly to a standstill by the freeze, are eerily silent. The best viewing place is from the top of the gorge; you can also walk right up to the canyon's edge above the waterfall, but take care on the wet rocks. Note that there are no substantial safety barriers at the site so be extremely careful, especially with kids.

Cafés and restaurants

Efstidalur

MAP PAGE 88, POCKET MAP V1
Route 37, about 15km east from Laugarvatn and Fontana Spa Ⓦ efstidalur.is.
Smart hotel restaurant surrounded by beautiful farmland, serving the best food in the region, much of it locally sourced. Try the smoked trout or beef soup, or a home-reared steak. KrKr

Friðheimar

MAP PAGE 88, POCKET MAP U3
806 Reykholt, Flúðir Ⓦ fridheimar.is.
Tomato fans rejoice, this farm-to-fork restaurant shines a light on the humble fruit. Think hand-rolled pasta with lashings of rich sauce or the signature Friðheimar soup mopped up with a wedge of oven-fresh bread, all washed down with a Bloody Mary of course. Meals are served in a huge greenhouse. KrKr

Gullfoss Visitor Centre

MAP PAGE 88, POCKET MAP V1
Gullfoss, by the car park and lookout Ⓦ gullfoss.is/cafe.
Timber-framed building with mountain views. Try its lamb stew; much else is ordinary and overpriced. KrKrKr

Restaurant Geysir Glíma

Gullfoss Visitor Centre

Minilik

MAP PAGE 88, POCKET MAP V2
Hrunamannavegur (Route 30), Flúðir
ℹ 846 9798.
Iceland's sole Ethiopian restaurant is loudly striped in green, yellow and red. Dishes are tangy, sour and spicy and served with traditional *njeera* (fermented dough pancakes) – try them with *awaze tibs* (a fried lamb dish). Plenty of vegetarian options, and excellent coffee. KrKr

Restaurant Geysir Glíma

MAP PAGE 88, POCKET MAP V1
At the Visitor Centre, Geysir Ⓦ geysirglima.is.
Despite the chic, Nordic-minimalist decor and its obvious tourist-trap potential, prices are pretty reasonable here. Expect light, easy meals like quiche and salad or a pizza. This was the site of Iceland's first wrestling school, hence the photo display. Kr

Skjól

MAP PAGE 88, POCKET MAP V1
Route 35, halfway between Geysir and Gullfoss ℹ 899 4541.
This dark timber, lodge-style bar, out in a lonely field between two of Iceland's most touristed attractions, is good for a convivial after-tour drink, though it also does tasty pizzas and grills if you're feeling hungry. Kr

The south coast and Heimaey

Heading east from Reykjavík, Highway 1 (the Ringroad) runs parallel to the coast for 185km through a well-watered region of rolling green pasture – home to Iceland's major horse stud farms – and down to the country's southernmost point near the pleasant seaside village of Vík. The final third of the journey passes within sight of the Eyjafjallajökull and Mýrdalsjökull ice caps; Eyjafjallajökull's 1666m apex is southwestern Iceland's highest point, and site of the volcanic eruption in 2010 which grounded aircraft across Europe. Along the way are hothouses at Hveragerði, some key saga landscapes, stunning waterfalls at Seljalandsfoss and Skógar, one of the country's best hiking trails, plus some bizarre black-sand beaches. Offshore, a ferry can whisk you over to impressive cliffs, volcanoes and puffin colonies at Heimaey, largest of the Westman Islands.

Hveragerði

MAP PAGE 94, POCKET MAP U2
Ringroad, 40km southeast of Reykjavík
Ⓦ south.is. Geothermal Park at
Hveramörk 13. Charge.

Sitting astride a patently active geothermal area, **Hveragerði**

Hveragerði Geothermal Park

comprises a compact grid of homes just north of the Ringroad, all overlooked by a crumpled mass of steaming hills. This was the first place in Iceland to harness underground heat for agriculture back in the 1920s, and almost half the buildings in town are **hothouses**, growing a year-round supply of fresh vegetables and garden plants. Other attractions include a **crevasse** which opened up during an earthquake in 2008 and today runs right through the tourist office and a **Geothermal Park** by the church, which sports steaming vents, bubbling mud pools and even a miniature geyser. Ask at the tourist office inside the shopping centre at the entrance to town about half-day **hiking trails** into the hills, where there are more hissing steam vents and a thermal stream in which you can enjoy a warm soak.

Selfoss

MAP PAGE 94, POCKET MAP U2
Ringroad, 57km southeast of Reykjavík;
Kerið crater is 15km north on Route 35.

The main landmark at **Selfoss**, a large service town on the fast-flowing Ölfusá, is its substantial **suspension bridge** (Ölfusárbrú), which first opened in 1891 and immediately drew business away from the small river ferry which used to operate downstream.

Homes and shops quickly began to spring up around the new crossing, and gradually Iceland's first inland town took shape. The original bridge – whose construction caused a major strike, after labourers were only given fresh salmon to eat – collapsed in 1944, though, when a pair of milk trucks tried to drive across it at the same time.

The bridge was rebuilt in under six months, reopening in 1945. Aside from this, the sole sight nearby is the dinky little **Kerið** crater, a 70m-deep, flooded volcanic depression formed from deep red scoria gravel.

Selfoss is also something of a gateway town for visitors: the Ringroad continues eastwards over the well-watered plains of the lower Þjórsá and Rangá river systems, while to the north, routes push on towards the Golden Circle and Interior.

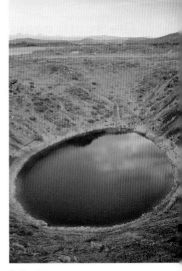

Kerið crater

Stokkseyri and Eyrarbakki

MAP PAGE 94, POCKET MAP U3
Route 34, 15km south of Selfoss. Ghost Centre at Hafnargata 9, Stokkseyri Ⓦicelandicwonders.is. Charge.

Insignificant today, these two pretty seaside villages have a rich historical heritage – and excellent **restaurants** (see page 101). The former fishing hamlet of **Stokkseyri** was once an important port, though when you stand on the stone storm wall and gaze out across the seaweed-strewn rocks and reefs, it's hard to imagine fishermen launching their heavy rowing boats from such an inhospitable shore. The old fish-processing factory incorporates a **Ghost Centre**, a slightly tacky take on Icelandic folklore.

About 4km west, larger **Eyrarbakki** houses a prison and an attractive core of old wooden homes, but is principally famous for being where Bjarni Herjólfsson set sail in 985 AD, on a voyage which took him within sight of North America (albeit accidentally). He later told Leifur Eiríksson about his discovery, and so it was Leifur who became the first known European to make

Stokkseyri has a rich historic heritage

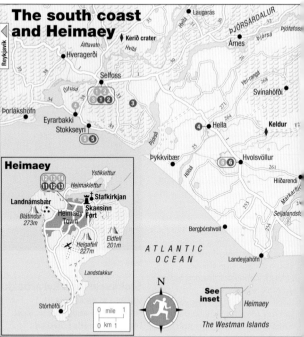

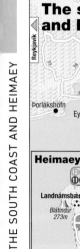

landfall in the Americas – or "Vinland" as he called it, after the vines that grew there.

Keldur

MAP PAGE 94, POCKET MAP V3
Off the Ringroad 95km southeast of Reykjavík, then 20km north on Route 264, the final few kilometres on a good gravel road. Charge.

Though a little off the beaten track, saga associations make the detour to **Keldur** a rewarding trip. This pretty farm sits amid fields on the edge of an overgrown lava flow, with the cloud-smudged **Hekla volcano** (see page 106) as a backdrop. Most of its buildings are recent, but the estate dates to Viking times and parts of a traditional turf-roofed block here might well be over eight hundred years old: the structural beams are dated to the seventeenth century, but wall panels are decorated with simple line engravings,

typical of the Viking period. Of similar vintage is the rough-hewn **tunnel** under the house (sometimes open to the public), which was built as an escape route in case of siege. It's believed that **Snorri Sturluson**, Iceland's great medieval man of letters, was raised at Keldur.

The Lava Centre

MAP PAGE 94, POCKET MAP V3
Austurvegur 14, Hvolsvöllur, Ringroad 100km southeast of Reykjavík
Ⓦ lavacentre.is. Charge.

The **Lava Centre**, housed in a long, low modernist building by the Ringroad, offers a fun and informative introduction to Iceland's geology and vulcanology. Interactive exhibits give a rundown of country's historic eruptions, earthquakes and lava spills – and the systems put in place to warn of future events. Southern volcanoes get the fullest

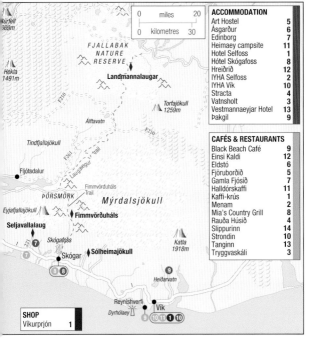

ACCOMMODATION	
Art Hostel	5
Ásgarður	6
Edinborg	7
Heimaey campsite	11
Hotel Selfoss	1
Hótel Skógafoss	8
Hreiðrið	12
IYHA Selfoss	2
IYHA Vík	10
Stracta	4
Vatnsholt	3
Vestmannaeyjar Hotel	13
Þakgil	9

CAFÉS & RESTAURANTS	
Black Beach Café	9
Einsi Kaldi	12
Eldstó	6
Fjöruborðið	5
Gamla Fjósið	7
Halldórskaffi	11
Kaffi-krús	1
Menam	2
Mia's Country Grill	8
Rauða Húsið	4
Slippurinn	14
Strondin	10
Tanginn	13
Tryggvaskáli	3

SHOP	
Víkurprjón	1

treatment: ever-murmuring Hekla, which last erupted in 2000; Katla (worryingly overdue for an eruption); and Eyjafjallajökull, whose 2010 ash cloud buried nearby farms, played havoc with European airlines, and caused amusement in Iceland as foreign newsreaders attempted to pronounce it. Surprisingly for a country with access to some incredible archive footage of these events, the cinema is slightly underwhelming – commentary would help – though the shots of oozing lava are impressive.

Seljalandsfoss

MAP PAGE 94, POCKET MAP V3
120km southeast of Reykjavík at the junction of the Ringroad and Route 249.
East from Hvolsvöllur, just past the turning to Landeyjahöfn and the ferry port for Heimaey (see page 100), Route 249 branches north towards Þórsmörk (see page 108). Almost immediately you reach **Seljalandsfoss**, an impressive **waterfall** that drops 60m off the long, undercut hillside into a shallow pool. There are good views from slopes off to one side, and a footpath runs

The Lava Centre

Njál's Saga

With its hardboiled narrative, a deep streak of dark humour and deadpan descriptions of shocking violence, **Njál's Saga** paints a vivid picture of clan warfare in tenth-century Iceland. The story centres on the life of the far-sighted Njál Þorgeirsson and his great friend, the heroic and generous Gunnar Hámundarson, whose lives are pitched against the evil schemings of Mörð Valgarðsson. Jealous of Gunnar's popularity, Mörð manipulates a succession of disreputable characters into picking fights with him, and Gunnar is eventually branded a troublemaker and exiled from Iceland at the Alþing law courts (see box, page 87). When he refuses to leave, a vengeful posse led by Mörð lays siege to his home, finally killing him after his spiteful wife refuses to help defend the house – inspiring Gunnar's memorable comment, "To each their own way of earning fame".

Meanwhile, encouraged by Mörð, Njál's sons carry out their own vendettas against a rival clan. After peace talks break down, Njál and almost his entire family are driven into their house and burned to death, an event which deeply divides the country. The sole survivor, Kári, chases "the Burners" overseas, where he hunts them down, one at a time. But his anger eventually subsides, and he makes a pilgrimage to seek absolution from the pope before returning to Iceland, where all the players in the saga finally make peace.

right behind the curtain – expect a good soaking from the spray. It's especially photogenic on summer evenings, when the low sun catches the spray and makes the falls glow gold. Walk along the cliff and you'll find several smaller falls too, one of which, **Gljúfrafoss**, is almost hidden inside the cliff-face.

Seljalandsfoss waterfall

Seljavallalaug swimming pool is fed by hot springs

Seljavallalaug

MAP PAGE 94, POCKET MAP W3
Ringroad 140km southeast of Reykjavík,
then north along gravel Route 242 for a
few kilometres to a parking area. Free.

Inland off the Ringroad, and then
a fifteen-minute walk along a
rubble-filled gorge, **Seljavallalaug**
is a fairly shallow, rectangular
swimming pool fed by a hot

Fimmvörðuháls hike

The 25km-long trail from **Skógar** (see page 98) to **Þórsmörk**
(see page 108), via the Fimmvörðuháls pass between the
Eyjafjallajökull and Mýrdalsjökull ice caps, is one of Iceland's best
– and most demanding – day hikes. It's usually accessible without
equipment from mid-June to September, though you always need
to come prepared for rain and snow, poor visibility and cold. The
track is erratically pegged, so be sure to carry a compass and a
suitable map.

From the top of Skógarfoss, the trail follows the river uphill past
many small **waterfalls**. Some 8km along there's a footbridge
and the landscape changes to a dark, rocky plain, gradually
climbing to snowfields. Along the way you pass **two hiking
huts** (you need to book beds via ⓦ utivist.is) and a pale blue tarn
at **Fimmvörðuháls** (1043m), the flat pass in between the two
glaciers. You end up at the top of a steep, 100m snowfield with
dramatic views down into Þórsmörk; the quickest way down is to
cautiously slide it on your backside. At the bottom is a short but
scary traverse across a narrow ledge to the flat, muddy plateau
of **Morinsheiði**, from where a relatively straightforward descent
lands you at Þórsmörk. Allow at least eight hours for the journey,
even in good weather.

spring. It was just about buried by ash in the 2010 Eyjafjallajökull eruption – though you can't see the ice cap itself from here, you're right under the edge of the Eyjafjallajökull plateau – but the pool is now clean again, and having an outdoor soak amid the wild, untamed scenery is a memorable and quintessentially Icelandic experience.

Skógar

MAP PAGE 94, POCKET MAP W4
Ringroad, 155km southeast of Reykjavík.
Folk Museum Ⓦ skogasafn.is. Charge.

There's very little to the hamlet of **Skógar** – not even a proper shop or fuel pump – and there'd be no reason to stop if it weren't for a stunning waterfall, plus an unusually interesting museum. Invisible from the road, the waterfall – **Skógarfoss** – is a 62m-high monster: stand in front of it (if the outward blast of air doesn't knock you over) and the world disappears amid roaring waters and spray. There's a metal staircase to the top and the start of the muddy moorland trail up over the mountains towards Þórsmörk

(see page 108), with long views seawards out to Heimaey.

Across the hamlet, Skógar's **Folk Museum** sketches out the region's history through an eclectic collection which takes in everything from nineteenth-century wooden fishing boats and turf farmhouses to a copy of the Bible dating from 1584, a Viking cloak pin, and a brass ring from a treasure chest which some stingy farmer – who didn't want his children to inherit his wealth – had thrown into the pool at Skógarfoss.

Sólheimajökull

MAP PAGE 94, POCKET MAP W3
153km southeast along the Ringroad from Reykjavík, then 5km north along the gravel Route 221.

Immediately over the shallow, glacier-fed Jökulsá Fúlilækur, turn north off the Ringroad and follow the track to a parking area. From here, it's a fifteen-minute walk to the front of **Sólheimajökull**, a narrow but substantial **glacier** descending off the Mýrdalsjökull ice cap. As they move under their own colossal weight, Iceland's glaciers grind the rocks below into black gravel and sand which

The roaring, 62m-high falls of Skógarfoss

View from Dyrhólaey

makes the ice tongues look "dirty", but Sólheimajökull is certainly impressive, deeply streaked in crevasses. Don't approach too close, as the glacier front is unstable.

Dyrhólaey

MAP PAGE 94, POCKET MAP W4
165km southeast along the Ringroad from Reykjavík, then 6km south on Route 218.
Dyrhólaey is Iceland's southernmost point, a dramatic set of basalt cliffs jutting out to sea over a long expanse of black sand. There's a lighthouse, and the cliffs are pierced by a huge arch – not visible from here, though *Black Beach Café* (see page 101) at Reynishverfi makes a fine vantage point – that is large enough for a yacht to pass beneath. Dyrhólaey's grassy tops are also riddled with puffin burrows, occupied by breeding birds throughout the summer.

Reynishverfi

MAP PAGE 94, POCKET MAP W4
175km southeast of the Ringroad from Reykjavík, then 6km south on Route 215.
East of Dyrhólaey the view is blocked by Reynisfjall, a ridge of hills running to the sea. At its southwestern tip lies **Reynishverfi**, an attractive shingle beach with treacherous waves (don't get too close) and a steep cliff faced in twisted basalt columns. Down the beach is a large cave, while the offshore stacks are the Troll Rocks, which are better viewed from Vík.

Vík

MAP PAGE 94, POCKET MAP X4
Ringroad, 185km southeast of Reykjavík.
A pretty coastal village caught between Reynisfjall's steep, sodden slopes and a deadening expanse of volcanic desert to the east, **Vík** started life as a trading station during the nineteenth century and has since expanded to fill a few streets. The village gained something of a celebrity status when it starred in Netflix's 2021 supernatural thriller series *Katla*, where ash-covered undead emerge from the ice following the eruption of a sub-glacial volcano. The only sight in town is **Brydebúð**, the original wooden general store around which Vík coalesced, which now serves as an information centre, local history museum,

Getting to Heimaey

The Herjólfur car and passenger **ferry** to Heimaey (🌐 herjolfur. is) departs several times a day from **Landeyjahöfn**, 15km south off the Ringroad at Seljalandsfoss (see page 95) via Route 254. For **flights from Reykjavík,** contact Eagle Air (🌐 eagleair.is); book online for discounted fares.

and a restaurant. The road runs 500m past Brydebúð and down to a parking bay above the sea, beyond which lies Reynisfjall's southernmost cliffs, packed with nesting seabirds, three tall spires offshore known as Reynisdrangar – the **Troll Rocks** – and a long, **black-sand beach** stretching eastwards to the horizon.

Heimaey

MAP PAGE 94, POCKET MAP V4
Eldheimar museum, Helgafellsbraut
🌐 eldheimar.is. Charge.

The volcanic **Westman Islands**, 10km off Iceland's southwest coast, all formed over the last few thousand years – though the youngest, Surtsey, popped out of the waves as recently as the 1960s.

The only inhabited island in the group, **Heimaey**, is also the largest at 6km long, and the ferry (see box, above) docks alongside fishing boats right in the middle of Heimaey town. Around the harbour, Skansinn is a reconstructed thirteenth-century stone fort, while **Stafkirkjan** is a traditional wooden church, built in the Viking style in 2000. Inland, paths lead through the rough mass of the Kirkjubærhraun lavafield and up to the summit of Eldfell volcano, whose 1973 eruption nearly destroyed the town. For more on this event, visit the superb **Eldheimar museum**, built around the excavated remains of a house which was completely buried under ash. To see puffins in the wild you'll need to hike 6km south to Stórhöfði headland, whose grassy slopes are riddled through summer with their burrows.

Stafkirkjan, a traditional wooden church in Heimaey

Eldstó is a pottery, gallery and café hybrid

Shop

Víkurprjón

MAP PAGE 94, POCKET MAP X4
Next to the N1 fuel station on the Ringroad,
Vík ⓦ icewear.is.

This factory outlet has made a
name for itself with the quality
of its woollens – everything from
traditional heavy-duty Icelandic
jumpers to hats, gloves and
blankets. The ground floor has all
the tourist tat; head upstairs for
outdoor wear and lower prices.

Cafés and restaurants

Black Beach Café

MAP PAGE 94, POCKET MAP W4
Reynishverfi ⓦ blackbeach.is.

A modern glass-fronted affair, built
of black basalt blocks and perfectly
camouflaged against the cliffs, this
makes a perfect spot to withdraw
from bad weather and enjoy a
warming bowl of lamb soup, fish
and chips or just a cake and coffee.
Don't miss the superb views down
the cragged coast to Dyrhólaey's
arch (see page 99). Kr

Einsi Kaldi

MAP PAGE 94
At the Vestmannaeyjar Hotel,
Vestmannabraut 28, Heimaey
ⓦ einsikaldi.is.

Smart and expensive restaurant
inside the town's only real hotel (see
page 119). Safe bets are the salted
cod, rack of lamb with thyme or
the mushroom wellington. If you
can't make up your mind, try the
three-course set menu, fair value at
9500kr. KrKrKr

Eldstó

MAP PAGE 94, POCKET MAP V3
Austurvegur 2, Hvolsvöllur ⓦ eldsto.is.

Pottery, gallery and café inside a
comfy, old-style timber-and-tin
building. Variable quality, but on a
good day the lamb soup or fish and
chips do the job well. The cake and
coffee is always good. KrKr

Fjöruborðið

MAP PAGE 94, POCKET MAP U3
Eyrarbraut 3a, Stokkseyri ⓦ fjorubordid.is.

Lobster restaurants have flourished
in Iceland over the past few years,

and this is one of the best – not least for the location, inside a wooden shack up against the sea wall at no-horse Stokkseyri village. It sells a whopping fifteen tons of lobster a year; a set meal of lobster soup, 300g of langoustine tails and a dessert costs 13,250Kr, but you could always just order the soup (3450Kr) or 250g of tails (8700Kr). KrKrKrKr

Gamla Fjósíð

MAP PAGE 94, POCKET MAP W3
Ringroad, about 10km west of Skógar
Ⓦ gamlafjosid.is.
Housed in a low-ceilinged former cowshed, this comfortable café-restaurant dishes up a range of tasty dishes – everything from burgers to vegetable curry to catch of the day. It's perhaps best known, though, for its "volcano soup", a beef stew laden with chillies. Kr

Halldórskaffi

MAP PAGE 94, POCKET MAP X4
Inside Brydebúð, Vík Ⓦ halldorskaffi.is.
About half of this old timber building is a dining room, but it still can't cope with the crowds who come for its superb pizzas: the seafood special with

shrimps, mussels and tuna is delicious. It doesn't take bookings, so be prepared to wait – it's worth it. KrKr

Kaffi-krús

MAP PAGE 94, POCKET MAP U2
Austurvegur, Selfoss Ⓦ kaffikrus.is.
One of the longest-running cafés outside the capital, this cosy, low-ceilinged place is best for fine coffee, cakes and light meals (eaten on the terrace in good weather), though it also does some pricey mains – burgers, salmon or grills. KrKr

Menam

MAP PAGE 94, POCKET MAP U2
Eyravegur 8, Selfoss Ⓦ menam.is.
The heat and spices are toned down a bit for local tastes, but *Menam*'s traditional Thai dishes, such as green chicken curry, are packed with flavour and are excellent value for money. Kr

Mia's Country Grill

MAP PAGE 94, POCKET MAP W4
Skógar Ⓣ 696 6542.
You can't miss this bright red polka-dot van serving fresh, crispy fried fish and chips. One of the best places to eat near Skógarfoss. Kr

A cosy corner at hotel-turned-restaurant *Tryggvaskáli*

Halldórskaffi is famed for its pizza

Rauða Húsið

MAP PAGE 94, POCKET MAP U3
Búðarstíg 4, Eyrarbakki ⓦ **raudahusid.is.**
Alternative to Stokkseyri's
Fjöruborðið (see page 101), though
there's a wider choice of dishes
besides lobster (which is also cheaper
here): fish of the day, lamb or cod
fillet with crab and squid ink risotto.
Don't miss the warm chocolate cake
spiked with spiced rum for dessert.
Booking essential. KrKrKr

Slippurinn

MAP PAGE 94
Strandvegur 76, Vestmannaeyjabær
ⓦ **slippurinn.com.**
Heimaey-born chef Gísli Matthías
Auðunsson Slippurinn offers
inventive tasting menus showcasing
local fare, much sourced from his
own kitchen-garden. Catch of the
day is served with foraged seaweed;
think sweet langoustine in *beurre
blanc* with sea truffle and an apple,
kohlrabi and sorrel salad. KrKrKr

Strondin

MAP PAGE 94, POCKET MAP X4
Austurvegur 18, Vík ☏ **487 1230.**
Facing seawards from behind the
N1 roadhouse, *Strondin* has an
outdoor terrace and glassed-in
dining room for wet days. Dishes
cover everything from Icelandic fish
stew to chicken pasta with basil and
tomato, best washed down with the
essential *brennevin* chaser. Kr

Tanginn

MAP PAGE 94
Tangagata, Heimaey ☏ **414 4420.**
Down at the harbour, this dark
room with feature windows and
heavy pine furniture makes a
surprisingly chic setting for feasting
on excellent seafood. The soup
is a soul-nourishing starter, best
followed by catch of the day or lamb
massaman – though it also serves a
not-very-traditional horse fillet. Kr

Tryggvaskáli

MAP PAGE 94, POCKET MAP U2
**Austere 1, on the roundabout by the bridge,
Selfoss** ⓦ **tryggvaskali.is.**
Hidden off the roundabout by the
bridge, the oldest wooden building
in Selfoss makes a quirky setting
for excellent food – slow-cooked
salmon and barley, lobster soup
or lamb with black garlic sauce.
Formerly a hotel, rooms are still
furnished with period fittings. KrKr

The Interior

You'd need to set aside a good week for a comprehensive trip across the heart of Iceland's Interior, a stark landscape of monochrome gravel plains, enormous ice caps and atrocious storms – but you can reach its fringes with an overnight visit. There are Viking remains at Þjórsádalur, a valley ravaged by the twelfth-century eruption of one of Iceland's most active volcanoes, Hekla; an extraordinary hot-spring bathing experience in the wilds at Landmannalaugar; and stunning highland scenery at Þórsmörk, whose horizons are hemmed in by glacier caps. With a little more time, it's also possible to walk between Landmannalaugar and Þórsmörk along one of the country's finest hiking trails – as long as you come equipped for the weather and a few relatively shallow river crossings.

Stöng

MAP PAGE 105, POCKET MAP W2

115km east from Ryekjavík via Selfoss (see page 92) and Route 32, then 7km north along Route 327, a gravel track that can sometimes be impassable for conventional vehicles.

Iceland's longest river – the Þjórsá – exits the Interior through **Þjórsárdalur**, a once fertile valley which in 1104 was smothered under a thick blanket of volcanic ash during an eruption of Hekla,

only a few kilometres to the east. Up on the valley's eastern side, ongoing excavations since the 1930s have uncovered the well-preserved remains of **Stöng**, the farmstead of Viking chieftain Gaukur Trándilsson. Protected inside a tin-roofed shed, stone foundations and postholes mark the outline of a longhouse, with the central fire pit, various halls, outhouses, animal pens and private quarters clearly visible. Not on

Þjóðveldisbærinn, a reconstructed period homestead

The Interior

```
0        miles        10
0      kilometres      15
```

Gullfoss

Laugarvatn

Háifoss

Sultartangalón

F26

Apavatn

Stöng

Flúðir

ÞJÓRSÁRDALUR

Þjóðveldisbærinn

F208

Laugarás

Árnes

Þjófafoss

Búrfell 669m

F225

FJALLABAK NATURE RESERVE

F208

Þjórsá

Reykjavík

Hekla 1491m

Landmannalaugar

Svínahöfði

F210

Hella

Keldur

Álftavatn

Torfajökull 1259m

F210

Þykkvibær

Hvolsvöllur

Hliðarendi

Tindfjallajökull

Fljótsdalur

Laugavegur Trail

Bergþórsvoll

The Saga Centre

Markarfljót

F261

F249

Mýrdalsjökull

ÞÓRSMÖRK

Eyjafjallajökull

Fimmvörðuháls

ATLANTIC OCEAN

Landeyjahöfn

Seljalandsfoss

Skógafoss

Fimmvörðuháls Trail

Skógar

N

ACCOMMODATION
Hiking hut   2, 3, 4, 5, 6
Leirubakki   1

view are an adjoining smithy and church, which were discovered only recently.

Háifoss

MAP PAGE 105, POCKET MAP W2
A 20km return hike from the car park at Stöng, or a 12km drive each way along gravel routes 327 and 332, which might be too rough for conventional vehicles.
Northeast up the valley from Stöng, **Háifoss** – Iceland's fourth-highest waterfall – plunges 120m off the Interior plateau in a single narrow curtain, the deep, narrow canyon below undercut by the force of the water. A second falls upstream is joined to the first by a short but narrow gully.

Þjóðveldisbærinn

MAP PAGE 105, POCKET MAP W2
115km east from Ryekjavík via Selfoss (see page 92) and Route 32, then 500m south along a signposted track
ⓦ thjodveldisbaer.is/en. Charge.
To appreciate how the longhouse at Stöng originally appeared, visit nearby **Þjóðveldisbærinn**, a reconstructed period homestead built from hand-cut timber and roofed in thick slabs of insulating turf. Inside, it's surprisingly cosy and warm (though don't forget that livestock were penned here too, at least through the winter), and the bright furnishings suggest a comfortable – if very public – living space.

Seasonal access

Most Interior roads are **four-wheel-drive only**, and even then are open for just a few months each summer, when they're covered by buses and private tours. Check sight accounts for details.

Hekla, on the horizon, is one of Iceland's most active volcanoes

Hekla

MAP PAGE 105, POCKET MAP W2
Contact Discover Iceland for guided hikes to the summit Ⓦ discover.is.

With its 1500m-high summit usually hidden by cloud, **Hekla** – one of Iceland's most active volcanoes – is named after an expression meaning "Hooded". The mountain's regular eruptions (including the one that buried Stöng in 1104), disturbing subterranean grumblings and a belief that its sulphurous crater formed the very entrance to hell, left it unclimbed until the eighteenth century; it last stirred in February 2000, when hundreds of sightseers from Reykjavík became trapped on Hekla's foothills by a snowstorm. On clear days, its hunchbacked crest dusted in snow makes an unmistakable landmark, visible from as far away as Selfoss.

Þjófafoss

MAP PAGE 105, POCKET MAP V2
123km east from Reykjavík via the Ringroad and Route 26, then 4km west on a good gravel track.

One of the best views to be had of Hekla is from **Þjófafoss**, a broad, lively waterfall just to the west, which sits below a looming flat-topped hill in a bend of the Þjórsá. You're not only close to Hekla here, but also surrounded by a strangely attractive monochrome landscape of degraded lava and pale yellow pumice pebbles. Despite the apparent desolation and the bumpy gravel road in, this isn't a particularly difficult place to reach, providing an easy taster of the Interior's barren charms.

Landmannalaugar

MAP PAGE 105, POCKET MAP W2
175km east from Reykjavík via the Ringroad, Route 26 and the F225. Route F225 is open June–September and is four-wheel-drive only, involving soft sand and several dangerous river crossings. For summer bus schedules, contact Trex (Ⓦ trex.is). Jeep day-tours are run by Landmannalaugar Tours (Ⓦ landmannalaugartours.com) and Arctic Adventures (Ⓦ adventures.is).

Set amid a rugged landscape of shattered obsidian and rhyolite peaks, brightly streaked in orange, grey and green, **Landmannalaugar** is a flat-bottomed gravel valley bordered on one side by a massive fifteenth-century lava flow. Out

Laugavegur hike

The superb **Laugavegur hiking trail** stretches 55km between Landmannalaugar and Þórsmörk, divided into stages by huts and campsites which are grouped at regular intervals. From Þórsmörk, you can continue south over the mountains to Skógar via the Fimmvörðuhals pass (see box, page 97).

The first stage (12km) passes a steaming thermal area at Stórihver – a bizarre sight amid the snow – before ending high in the hills at **Hrafntinnusker**, a weather-beaten slope covered in obsidian boulders. From here it's another 12km over a snowy rhyolite plateau and down a steep slope to **Álftavatn**, a small lake set amid vivid green hillocks; the next stage is slightly longer and crosses a gravel desert and a couple of very shallow (but icy cold) rivers to a tiny sheltered valley at **Bótnar-Emstrur**. There are fabulous views of Entujökull, the nearest of Mýrdalsjökull's glaciers, from clifftops around 3km southeast of the hut here. The final 15km leg to **Þórsmörk** (see page 108) is over relatively dull moorland before you ford the Þröngá – the deepest river you have to ford on the trail – and enter the suddenly lush birch and juniper woodland at Þórsmörk's northern boundary, just a short walk from the huts and bus stop.

The trail is open from June until mid-September, when buses run daily from Reykjavík to the end points at Landmannalaugar and Þórsmörk (see ⓦ trex.is for bus schedules). Hikers need to carry their own food and be fully equipped for the weather conditions. For information, contact the Icelandic Touring Association (ⓦ fi.is).

from underneath the lava emerge two streams, one icy cold and the other scalding hot; there's a perfect wild bathing spot where the waters mix. Known for its summer pasture, Landmannalaugar was once a staging post on cross-Iceland roads,

and there are some fine day-hikes in the vicinity – in good weather, don't miss the chance to ascend **Bláhnúkur** (945m), the bald peak to the south, for spectacular views. There's a clearly marked path up the north face to the top, but for

Laugavegur has superb hiking

Þórsmörk, a scenic highland valley

a bit of excitement, try a slip-slide descent via the loose scree slopes to the west. For many, however, Landmannalaugar's appeal is in its location at the trailhead for the long-distance Laugavegur hiking route to Þórsmörk and the coast at Skógar.

Þórsmörk

MAP PAGE 105, POCKET MAP W3
155km southeast from Reykjavík via Route 1 and the F249. The F249 is four-wheel-drive only, involving rough gravel and dangerous river crossings, and is only open June–September. For bus schedules contact

Krossá River, Þórsmörk

Trex (W trex.is). Jeep tours run by Midgard Adventure (W midgardadventure.is).

A beautiful highland valley, **Þórsmörk** has hiking trails running in all directions, and thick stands of dwarf willow, birch and wildflowers watered by a web of glacial rivers that flow west off the Mýrdalsjökull ice cap. The valley is split into three areas, each with its own hiking hut accommodation; isolated on the far western side is Húsadalur (W volcanohuts.com), Þórsmörk's main bus terminus but still a thirty-minute hike from the main valley. This is split in two by the 7km-long Krossá River, a braided glacial flow which originates in the ice caps that hem everything in; to the north of the river is Þórsmörk proper, with a base of sorts at Skagfjörðsskáli hut (W fi.is), while to the south is Goðaland and Básar hut (W utivist. is). Be sure to cross the Krossá via the bridge; the river is dangerously cold and fast, and people have drowned trying to wade over. The best views on the river's north side are from the top of knuckle-like Valahnúkur, a brief hike up on a well-marked path; south of the Krossá lies a more challenging climb in the shape of 805m-hig Útigönguhöfði – the final section is incredibly steep, with chains to help you.

Þórsmörk hikes

Þórsmörk is covered in a network of excellent **hiking trails**, though these are not well marked on the ground and even "easy" routes tend to involve steep gradients, loose scree and occasionally high, narrow traverses. Rangers at the accommodation huts can provide useful maps, weather forecasts and general advice, though – hardened as they are to local conditions – they often underestimate potential difficulties.

The main walk from the **Skagfjörðsskáli** hut starts at the next bay east at Slyppugil, a wooded gully which you follow uphill to the jagged east–west ridge of Tindfjöll. The trail weaves along Tindfjöll's gravelly, landslip-prone north face to the solitary spire of Tröllakirkja, before emerging onto open heathland at Tindfjöll's eastern end: the double-tipped cone 2km northeast is Rjúpnafell, which you can climb via a steep, zigzagging path up to its 824m summit – give yourself at least five hours for the return hike from the hut.

The best excursion from the **Básar** hut is to follow the popular trail south towards Skógar (see page 98) as far as the flat, muddy Morinsheiði Plateau. From here you turn west and descend to a low saddle below 805m-high Útigönguhöfði, then take a hideously steep path straight up it to the rounded peak. Views from the top are breathtaking, and there's a chain to help your descent off the far side. A low, 5km-long ridge continues west to the heights directly above Básar, with an easy descent along a path to your starting point. Again, allow around five hours for the hike.

Hiking in Þórsmörk

ACCOMMODATION

Grand Reykjavík

Accommodation

Although Reykjavík's accommodation options continue to mushroom as the tourist influx increases, pressure on beds in the summer months is always great and it's a good idea to book in advance, especially in June, July and August. Hotels do not come cheap in Reykjavík, usually hovering around 25,000–35,000kr for an average double room in high season. The quality is, however, generally high, though rooms can be block-like and characterless – sometimes it's the view or the location that makes it. Online discounts and opting for a shared bathroom (where available) can reduce prices significantly. Guesthouses cost around 15,000–20,000kr; often family run, they tend to have more character than hotels, with rooms ranging from the barely furnished to the very comfortable, and facilities are usually shared. Prices overall tend to rise by around a third during the high season (May to September); those given here are for the cheapest double room during the summer months. At hostels, you'll find that meals are sometimes offered, though most have kitchens for self-catering. Campsites vary in size but will always have washing facilities, and sometimes a kitchen, too. Self-catering is worth considering since it will save a lot of money on eating out – one of the main expenses in Iceland.

Lækjartorg, Austurstræti and Austurvöllur

BORG MAP PAGE 28, POCKET MAP D4. Pósthússtræti 11 ⊕ hotelborg.is. The city's very first hotel, opened in the 1930s and the unofficial home of visiting heads of state ever since. A showcase of sophistication and four-star elegance, each room is individually decorated in Art Deco style with period furniture – and prices to match. It's hard to beat the location, too, right in the heart of the Austurvöllur area, with Austurstræti and Hafnarstræti right on the doorstep. KrKrKrKr

Accommodation price codes

Throughout the Guide, accommodation is categorized according to a price code, which roughly corresponds to the following price ranges. Price categories reflect the cost of a double room, without breakfast, in peak season.

Kr	under 10,000Kr
KrKr	10,000–18,000Kr
KrKrKr	18–35,000Kr
KrKrKrKr	over 35,000Kr

PLAZA MAP PAGE 28, POCKET MAP C3.
Aðalstræti 4 ⓦ centerhotels.com. The style
in this tastefully renovated old building, a
stone's throw from Austurstræti, is Nordic
minimalism meets old-fashioned charm,
with heavy wooden floors, plain white
walls and immaculately tiled bathrooms
complementing the high-beamed ceilings.
The rooms at the front of the hotel look
out over Ingolfstorg which can be noisy so
it may be wise to seek out a room further
back. KrKrKrKr

RADISSON BLU 1919 MAP PAGE 28,
POCKET MAP D3. Pósthússtræti 2
ⓦ radissonblu.com/1919hotel-reykjavik.
Housed in the elegant former headquarters
of the Eimskip shipping line, this Art Deco
hotel combines old-fashioned charm with
modern chic. Book one month in advance
to secure the best rates available. The
penthouse suites with elevated sleeping
sections and separate dining area are the
finest Reykjavík has to offer and would
make an ideal treat for a special occasion.
KrKrKrKr

REYKJAVÍK CENTRUM MAP PAGE
28, POCKET MAP C4. Aðalstræti 16
ⓦ islandshotel.is/hotels-in-iceland/hotel-
reykjavik-centrum. Built in traditional
early-1900s style, this hotel offers a
curious yet pleasing mix of stylish and
homely, featuring old-fashioned wallpapers
and fittings. Perfectly located on Aðalstræti,
it's near the action of Laugavegur as well as
being ideally situated for a gentle evening
stroll around Tjörnin, which is right on the
doorstep. KrKrKrKr

The harbour
THE REYKJAVÍK EDITION MAP PAGE
41, POCKET MAP E2. Austurbakki 2
ⓦ marriott.com. Iceland's first five-star
hotel has descended on Reykjavík: the
latest of Marriott's luxurious Edition hotels
rubs shoulders with the Harpa concert
hall on the Old Harbour. A charcoal-hued
timber exterior nods to local lava fields,
while inside cool Nordic interiors are
given a touch of drama by designer Ian
Schrager. The *Tides* restaurant, helmed by
chef Gunnar Karl Gíslason, showcases the
natural bounty of the island through playful

pairings like habaneros-spiked salmon or
rye bread-flavoured ice cream with foraged
blueberries. KrKrKrKr

REYKJAVÍK MARINA MAP PAGE
41, POCKET MAP B1. Mýrargata 2
ⓦ icelandhotelcollectionbyberjaya.
com. Bold, bright and refreshingly quirky,
this harbourside hotel not only enjoys
terrific views of the trawlers in dry dock
right outside, but its rooms also have a
maritime feel with a twist of chic. If you're
on a stopover deal with Icelandair (see
box, page 122), or are simply booking
accommodation via the airline and are
able to choose between this hotel and
the *Icelandair Reykjavík Natura* (see page
116), make this one your preference.
KrKrKrKr

Tjörnin and around
BALDURSBRÁ MAP PAGE 47, POCKET
MAP D7. Laufásvegur 41 ☎ 552 6646.
Another of Reykjavík's long-standing
accommodation options, this friendly,
modern guesthouse enjoys a fantastic
location, right in the city centre and
overlooking Tjörnin. Though the price is
good, rooms are a little cramped and the
floral decor may not be to everyone's taste.
The secluded garden with a hot tub for
guests' use is, however, a definite boon and
it's hard to find such a central location at
this price. KrKrKr

HOLT MAP PAGE 47, POCKET MAP E6.
Bergstaðastræti 37 ⓦ holt.is. First opened
in 1965, this is one of the most elegant and
luxurious hotels in Reykjavík. With over
three hundred paintings by Icelandic artists
adorning the rooms and public areas, it's a
little like staying overnight in an art gallery.
Rooms are of the Persian-carpet, dark-
wood-panelling, red-leather-armchair and
chocolate-on-the-pillow variety. KrKrKrKr

RADISSON BLU SAGA REYKJAVÍK MAP
PAGE 47, POCKET MAP M2. Hagatorg
ⓦ radissonblu.com/sagahotel-reykjavik.
This large, swanky business hotel is usually
packed with conference delegates dashing
up to admire the view from the top-floor
restaurant. The rooms are cosmopolitan in
feel and design, and feature bureaux and

comfortable armchairs. Book early for the best rates. Bear in mind that it's a good thirty-minute walk from here to the shops and restaurants on Laugavegur. KrKrKrKr

Bankastræti and around

FRÓN MAP PAGE 54, POCKET MAP F5. Laugarvegur 22A ⓦ hotelfron.is. If you're self-catering, this hotel right in the city centre should be your first choice. In addition to regular double rooms, it offers stylish, modern studios and larger apartments, each with bath, kitchenette and TV. Not only that, but the Bónus supermarket, offering the best prices on food and vegetables in town, is just across the road – perfect for when it comes to buying supplies. KrKrKr

KEX HOSTEL REYKJAVÍK MAP PAGE 54, POCKET MAP J5. Skúlagata 28 ⓦ kexhostel.is. Cool hostel in a converted biscuit factory overlooking the harbour, with a buzzy bar, restaurant and lounge. The vibe is cosy and lived in: walls plastered with maps, shelves groaning beneath the weight of books and antiques, and battered leather couches. Regular live music lures locals through the door, with everything from jazz to hip hop on the agenda. Dorm rooms are simple but comfortable. Dorms Kr, doubles KrKr

KLÖPP MAP PAGE 54, POCKET MAP F4. Klapparstígur 26 ⓦ centerhotels. is. Despite its bizarre name, this is one of central Reykjavík's better hotels and a sound choice: modern throughout, with all rooms boasting tasteful wooden floors, oak furniture and wall panelling. Rooms can be a little on the small side, though, so it probably pays to ask to look at more than one if you're not happy with your allocation. The breakfast room is also a little cramped. KrKrKrKr

REYKJAVÍK LOFT HOSTEL MAP PAGE 54, POCKET MAP E4. Bankastræti 7 ⓦ hostel. is. A lively hostel with an unparalleled location right in the thick of things and a jam-packed calendar of events, from karaoke sessions to food pop-ups and game nights. There are six- to eight-bed dorms as well as private rooms, plus a top-floor bar and roof terrace offering great views over the city centre. What's more, it's affiliated to HI, so there are discounts for members. Dorms Kr, doubles KrKrKr

ROOM WITH A VIEW MAP PAGE 54, POCKET MAP F5. Laugavegur 18 ⓦ roomwithaview.is. Quite simply, this place has got it right, offering a great selection of studios and apartments, all located on the sixth floor, overlooking the main shopping street, with incredible panoramic views from the shared balcony. Discount for stays of seven nights or more. KrKrKrKr

SKJALDBREIÐ MAP PAGE 54, POCKET MAP F5. Laugavegur 16 ⓦ centerhotels. is. This hotel is another of Reykjavík's long-standing options and it's hard to beat on several counts. True, the plain rooms sporting classic Nordic decor may be rather uninspiring, but the price for such a central location is fairly competitive: bars, restaurants and shops are all right outside your window. Note, too, that the windows have extra sound-proofing – especially needed on raucous Friday and Saturday nights on Laugavegur. KrKrKrKr

Hallgrímskirkja and around

FOSSHÓTEL BARON MAP PAGE 62, POCKET MAP J5. Barónsstígur 2–4 ⓦ islandshotel.is/hotels-in-iceland/ fosshotel-baron. Another good choice if you're thinking of doing a bit of self-catering, as there are microwaves in most of the en-suite doubles and studios. Throughout, the decor is neutral and modern, if unsensational, and many rooms have sea views. The thirty-plus apartments vary greatly in size, so look before you choose. Discounts for stays of three nights and over. Doubles KrKrKr, studios KrKrKrKr

FOSSHÓTEL LIND MAP PAGE 62, POCKET MAP K7. Rauðarárstígur 18 ⓦ islandshotel. is/hotels-in-iceland/fosshotel-lind. Bright, modern and functional hotel offering discounts for stays of three nights or more, and worth considering if other more central places are fully booked. Rooms are plainly decorated and unadventurous, but the location's within easy reach of Hlemmur's buses which bring the city centre to within a brief bus ride, instead of a twenty- to thirty-minute walk. KrKrKrKr

FOSSHÓTEL REYKJAVÍK MAP PAGE 62, POCKET MAP P2. Þórunnartún 1 ⓦ islandshotel.is/hotels-in-iceland/fosshotel-reykjavik.
Sprawling over sixteen floors, the *Fosshótel* chain's jewel in the crown opened for business back in 2015 and is Iceland's biggest hotel, boasting 320 guest rooms, all with magnificent views over the city's rooftops and the waterfront. Rooms are sleek and elegant, there's a spa and a gym, and even a pub with a great choice of beers. Be under no illusion, though – none of this comes cheap. KrKrKrKr

GUESTHOUSE 101 MAP PAGE 62, POCKET MAP K6. Laugavegur 101 ⓦ guesthouse101.is.
What makes this guesthouse worth considering is its location – it's roughly a fifteen-minute walk along Laugavegur into the centre and on to Lækjartorg; or there's the Hlemmur bus interchange right outside the door for longer journeys or tired legs. Prices are also reasonable, but otherwise it's a rather soulless place with cheap furniture and cell-like rooms. KrKrKr

LEIFUR EIRÍKSSON MAP PAGE 62, POCKET MAP G7. Skólavörðustígur 45 ⓦ hotelleifur.is.
It's hard to imagine a hotel with such a perfect location – step outside the door and you're right in front of the Hallgrímskirkja, with all Reykjavík has to offer a short stroll down Skólavörðustígur. It's a small, friendly and neatly furnished place to boot; the top-floor rooms, built into the sloping roof, are particularly worthwhile for their excellent views. KrKrKrKr

LUNA MAP PAGE 62, POCKET MAP F6. Spítalastígur 1 (Check in at Baldursgata 36) ⓦ luna.is.
If you're looking for spacious, beautifully decorated and superbly appointed apartments, this is the place to come. With modern and bright studios sleeping two people and larger apartments, also for two people, with high-quality fittings, this is a real home from home. There's also a three-room penthouse for rent. Studios KrKrKr, apartments KrKrKrKr

ÓÐINSVÉ MAP PAGE 62, POCKET MAP F6. Þórsgata 1 ⓦ odinsve.is.
Long-established place that's stylish, relaxed and within an easy trot of virtually everything – Skólavörðustígur and Laugavegur, for example, are barely five minutes' walk away. The elegantly decorated rooms have wooden floors, neutral decor, comfortable Scandinavian-style furniture, and feature work by renowned Icelandic photographer RAX. A pretty fair deal, especially given the way other hotels have raised their rates recently. KrKrKrKr

REYKJAVIK4YOU APARTMENT HOTEL MAP PAGE 62, POCKET MAP E5. Bergstaðastræti 12 ⓦ reykjavik4you.com.
Not much to fault here: good-sized, comfortable and fully furnished modern apartments (with well-equipped kitchens) just moments from Laugarvegur, Hallgrímskirkja and the centre of town. It's typical of a new wave of accommodation springing up in response to the sudden boom in tourism since 2010, which is beginning to undermine (or complement) the more traditional high-end hotels. KrKrKrKr

REYKJAVÍK DOWNTOWN HOTEL MAP PAGE 62, POCKET MAP F6. Skólavörðustígur 42 ⓦ reykjavikdowntownhotel.is.
Although this place likes to think it's a hotel, it's actually an upmarket guesthouse; the smart rooms all boast a kitchenette, though some share facilities. The location is also one of its best features, with Hallgrímskirkja as its next-door neighbour. KrKrKrKr

Öskjuhlíð and around

BUS HOSTEL REYKJAVÍK MAP PAGE 67, POCKET MAP N3. Skógarhlíð 10 ⓦ bushostelreykjavik.com.
Bargainous crash-pad in a former bus terminal near Reykjavík's domestic airport. Relaxed and breezy – think hiking boots piled at the front door, waterproof jackets slung across bedframes – with a convivial lounge and bar. Perfect for backpackers, with buses departing from right outside the front door

for the Blue Lagoon and the Golden Circle. Dorms Kr, doubles KrKr

FOSSHÓTEL RAUÐARÁ MAP PAGE 67, POCKET MAP N3. Rauðarárstígur 37 ⓦ islandshotel.is/hotels-in-iceland/fosshotel-raudara. Though featuring widely on online booking sites – which can throw up some exceptionally good deals – this is a rather functional and uninspiring hotel, roughly twenty minutes' walk from the centre. The plain and simple rooms are clean and presentable, though you might find some disturbingly orange furnishings in them. Book in advance for the best rate quoted here. KrKrKr

REYKJAVÍK NATURA MAP PAGE 67, POCKET MAP N3. Nauthólsvegur 52 ⓦ icelandhotelcollectionbyberjaya.com. A busy and impersonal hotel stuffed with stopover travellers (see box, page 122). The 200-odd rooms here are nice enough, with wooden floors and comfortable modern furnishings throughout, though are on the small side. For some people, the location will be too far from the centre – it really is a bit of a trek into the centre, under subways and over bridges (30–40min), and in the evenings and at weekends buses here are rather infrequent. Free access to the hotel spa. KrKrKrKr

SNORRI MAP PAGE 67, POCKET MAP N3. Snorrabraut 61 ⓦ snorrisguesthouse.com. This pebble-dashed modern block is not one of Reykjavík's most alluring, and the rooms are rather uninspiring, too. But the location is a winner, just a short walk (10–15min) from the centre, and there's a choice of shared facilities or en suite. The hotel is also on many of the city's bus routes, which means you will be able to get around quite easily should you base yourself here. KrKrKr

Eastern Reykjavík
ARCTIC COMFORT MAP PAGE 72, POCKET MAP Q3. Síðumúli 19 ☎ 588 5588. Oddly located in a business district a good walk (30–40min) from the centre, it's worth considering this place only when everything else is full. Its out-of-town location is not great, but it is perfectly smart and clean and offers good value for money. Some rooms have self-catering facilities. Several bus routes pass close by. KrKrKr

CABIN MAP PAGE 72, POCKET MAP P2. Borgartún 32 ⓦ hotelcabin.is. The best rooms in this good-value place are at the front, offering great views out over the sea and Mount Esja. Warm autumn colours throughout, with lots of browns and greys making the decor pleasant and restful. The cheaper double rooms are only ten square metres in size and can feel a little cramped. Though it's a good twenty- to thirty-minute walk into the centre, there is a bus stop right outside the hotel. KrKrKr

GRAND REYKJAVÍK MAP PAGE 72, POCKET MAP P2. Sigtún 38 ⓦ booking.com. The clue's in the name: there's no shortage of opulence here, with marble floors, stylish chrome fittings and wood panels aplenty, though for the money you may wish to be closer to the centre – it's a 25-minute walk from here. Accommodation is in two buildings – the original and a newer, shimmering high-rise tower whose rooms enjoy stunning views. KrKrKrKr

HILTON REYKJAVÍK NORDICA MAP PAGE 72, POCKET MAP P3. Suðurlandsbraut 2 ⓦ reykjavik.nordica.hilton.com. The *Hilton* chain's one and only hotel in Iceland is big on Nordic minimalism: glass, chrome and natural wood are everywhere you look. Rooms at the front of the sprawling building

Booking ahead
In order to get the lowest room rate book well in advance via the hotel's own website or try one of the many online booking sites. If you do arrive at the last minute without a reservation, the city tourist office may be able to help at its office on Laugavegur (see page 129). Alternatively, think about staying in Hafnarfjörður (see page 117), where pressure on beds is less intense.

enjoy views over the sea to Mount Esja. The hotel is popular with tour groups so it can feel rather anonymous given the number of guests here at any one time. KrKrKrKr

ÍSLAND MAP PAGE 72, POCKET MAP Q3. Ármúli 9 ⓦ booking.com. Though it tends to change hands fairly frequently due to its out-of-town location, this is another of Reykjavík's long-standing and dependable accommodation options. Although a little too far from the centre to be your first choice (about 2.5km), the light and airy Scandinavian-designed rooms, with lots of wood panels, glass and chrome, make this worth considering if others are full. KrKrKrKr

KRÍUNES MAP PAGE 72, POCKET MAP R4. Vatnsendi, Kríunesvegi 12 ⓦ kriunes. is. With your own transport, it's worth considering this great little guesthouse located a fifteen-minute drive southeast of the city. A former farmhouse painted in warm Mediterranean colours and sporting lovely terracotta tiles and wooden floors, it certainly lives up to its name: sited beside the "end of the water", it enjoys a truly fantastic lakeside location, surrounded by high trees and with views of the water. KrKrKr

REYKJAVÍK CAMPSITE MAP PAGE 72, POCKET MAP Q2. Sundlaugarvegur 32 ⓦ reykjavikcampsite.is. This is the cheapest place to stay in Reykjavík, with cooking and shower facilities on site, plus some rather small two-berth cabins with bunk beds; facilities are shared. The site is perfectly located for Iceland's biggest and best swimming pool, Laugardalslaug. The city centre, though, is a good walk away (30–40min) so it might be worth considering taking the bus if you want to save your legs. Camping Kr, cabins KrKrKr

Hafnarfjörður and around
HAFNARFJÖRÐUR CAMPING MAP PAGE 77. Hjallabraut 51 ⓦ lavahostel.is/ camping. Located within leafy Víðistaðatún park, off Flókagata north of the centre, the town's quiet campsite can make a nice alternative to the much bigger and busier site in Reykjavík. It's located in a quiet spot, has access to showers, and hot and cold

running water, though for other facilities campers must use Lava Hostel next door. Mid-May to mid-Sept. Kr

HELGUHÚS MAP PAGE 77. Lækjarkinn 8 ⓔ helguhus@helguhus.is. Named after the owner, Helga, this is one of the town's oldest accommodation options. It's a friendly, family-run guesthouse, and you'll be made to feel straight at home. There's just a handful of rather small and plainly decorated rooms which all share facilities, though there is access to a well-stocked kitchen should you choose to go self-catering. Note there's a three-night minimum stay. KrKrKrKr

HÓTEL VIKING MAP PAGE 77. Strandgata 55 ⓦ fjorukrain.is. If you're looking to get your Valhalla fix, this is the place to come. The 41 en-suite rooms bristle with over-the-top Viking decor, featuring lots of heavy wooden flourishes and gothic prints hanging on the walls. Next door to the main hotel there are also fourteen new six-bed cabins. Guests have use of a sauna and hot tub. Doubles KrKrKr, cabins KrKrKrKr

LAVA HOSTEL MAP PAGE 77. Hjallabraut 51 ⓦ lavahostel.is. This hostel is one of Hafnarfjörður's best-value options and makes a sound choice if you're looking for somewhere cheaper than Reykjavík. It's housed in a handsome modern timber structure next to the campsite and offers compact dorms (sleeping 4–8) as well as regular double rooms. Both dorms and rooms share facilities and look out over the park. Dorms Kr, doubles KrKrKr

The Reykjanes Peninsula
NORTHERN LIGHT INN MAP PAGE 81, POCKET MAP S3. 1 Northern Lights Road, off the Blue Lagoon approach road ⓦ nli. is. This long building is half-hidden amid moss-covered lava flows, located just minutes from the Blue Lagoon. Rooms are plain but comfortable, there's a cosy lounge area with large fireplace, and the views from the restaurant are great. KrKrKrKr

STRANDARKIRKJA CAMPSITE MAP PAGE 81, POCKET MAP T3. Strandarkirkja road, off Route 427. No phone. Spacious, grassy site close to the sea at this no-horse hamlet, run by a farmer who has installed showers, toilets, washing-up sinks and picnic tables. Kr

The Golden Circle

SKJÓL MAP PAGE 88, POCKET MAP V1. On Route 35, halfway between Geysir and Gullfoss ☎ 899 4541. Perfectly pitched between two of the country's most famous sights, there's a large campsite here, plus nine simple hostel-style rooms (all with shared facilities) with a separate restaurant/bar on hand. Kr

The south coast and Heimaey

ART HOSTEL MAP PAGE 94, POCKET MAP U3. Hafnargata 9, Stokkseyri, above the old fish factory ⓦ arthostel.is. A much cosier, more comfortable place than you'd guess from the storm-battered exterior, with a range of well-furnished dorms and doubles – some with en suites and kitchenettes. Good sea views. Dorms Kr, doubles KrKr

ÁSGARÐUR MAP PAGE 94, POCKET MAP V3. Hvolstrod, Hvolsvöllur, off the Ringroad up Route 261, beside the church ⓦ asgardurinn.is. Tucked into a thin belt of woodland, there's a handful of comfortable cabins here which sleep up to four, each complete with self-contained bathroom and kitchen. Camping also available. KrKr

EDINBORG MAP PAGE 94, POCKET MAP W3. Lambafell, Route 242 on the Seljavallalaug road ☎ 487 1212. This tin-sided building contains a range of comfortable en-suite twins and family rooms; the clean lines and timber furnishings are smart but it's the surrounding wild scenery that is the real attraction. KrKrKr

HEIMAEY CAMPSITE MAP PAGE 94. 1km west of town at Herjólfsdalur ☎ 846 9111. This site enjoys a spectacular location inside the collapsed bowl of an extinct volcano, with the grassy pitches half-encircled by high cliffs. Kr

HOTEL SELFOSS MAP PAGE 94, POCKET MAP U2. Eyravegi 2, Selfoss, close to the bridge ⓦ hotelselfoss.is. If you're after a "proper" multi-storey hotel with smart rooms and conference facilities, look no further than this dark block at the entrance to town. A good alternative to similar options in Reykjavík. KrKrKrKr

HÓTEL SKÓGAFOSS MAP PAGE 94, POCKET MAP W4. Skógar, on the falls road ⓦ hotelskogafoss.is. Long, single-storey building whose seventeen en-suite rooms are tidy and spacious, if a bit bland. Big breakfasts are available too, and you're just a short walk from the falls. KrKrKrKr

HREIÐRIÐ MAP PAGE 94. Corner of Faxastígur and Heiðarvegur ⓦ tourist.eyjar.is. The owner of this budget guesthouse has lived on Heimaey for decades and knows all the island's secret spots. Rooms are on the small side and facilities are shared. KrKr

IYHA SELFOSS MAP PAGE 94, POCKET MAP U2. Austurvegur 28 (the Ringroad), Selfoss ⓦ hostel.is. Occupying a renovated old house close to the bus stop, this well-equipped hostel has slightly spartan dorms, a kitchen, small hot tub and handy café. Dorms Kr

IYHA VÍK MAP PAGE 94, POCKET MAP X4. Suðurvíkurvegur 5, Vík, up near the church ⓦ hostel.is. This friendly, well-equipped hostel is very popular (in spite of its slightly stuffy dorms) and boasts a modern kitchen, plus a dining room with sea views. Dorms Kr

STRACTA MAP PAGE 94, POCKET MAP V3. Rangárflatir 4, Hella, on the coastal side of Route 1 ⓦ stractahotel.is. This large, modern, disorienting complex has corridors heading off in all directions. The rooms and apartments sport wooden floors, smart bathrooms and lots of white, with a clutch of on-site hot tubs and saunas. KrKrKrKr

VATNSHOLT MAP PAGE 94, POCKET MAP U3. Follow signposts 15km southeast of Selfoss via Route 305 ⓦ hotelvatnsholt.is. Located on a farm, this large guesthouse offers a choice of accommodation spread between several buildings, with and without en-suite facilities. There's a plethora of pets too, including an arctic fox and a raven. KrKrKr

VESTMANNAEYJAR HOTEL MAP PAGE 94. Vestmannabraut 28 Ⓦ hotel vestmannaeyjar.is. A modern, welcoming venue whose spacious guest rooms feature polished wooden floors and leather lounges; there's a hot tub for guests too. KrKrKr

ÞAKGIL MAP PAGE 94, POCKET MAP X4. Turn inland 5km east of Vík at Höfðabrekka and follow the slow, twisting gravel Route 214 for 17km Ⓦ thakgil.is. Isolated valley cradling a campsite and dotted with self-contained cabins with bunks sleeping up to four. There's also a communal dining area inside a large cave, and local hiking trails. June–Aug only. Camping Kr, cabins KrKrKr

The Interior

HIKING HUTS MAP PAGE 105, POCKET MAP W2–W4. Landmannalaugar, Laugavegur and Þórsmörk Ⓦ fi.is and Ⓦ utivist.is. These huts are like giant communal chalets with large kitchens, toilets, showers and basic sleeping arrangements in bunks or on mattresses on the floor. Bring sleeping bags and food, and book ahead online – you can't just turn up. Kr

LEIRUBAKKI MAP PAGE 105, POCKET MAP V2. Route 26 Ⓦ leirubakki.is. This hotel and restaurant has Hekla's snow-smudged summit for a backdrop. Don't miss the outdoor lava-block "Viking Pool", which is tepid but affords great views of the mountain. The only downside is that it can get crowded with noisy tour groups. Dorms Kr, doubles KrKrKr

ESSENTIALS

Norðurgarði Lighthouse

Arrival

You're most likely to arrive in Iceland at Keflavík International Airport, within a short bus ride of the capital, but there are a couple of other possibilities, depending on where you're coming from.

By air

Keflavík International Airport
(KEF; S2; ⓦkefairport.is), Iceland's major arrivals hub, is 40km west of the capital via the multi-lane Route 41 expressway. It's a small, uncomplicated affair and you'll most likely be through passport control and in the arrivals hall within half an hour or so of landing; note that the duty-free shop is by far the cheapest place to buy spirits in Iceland. There are a number of ATMs in the arrivals lobby.

Taxis to the city wait outside the airport but it's a good idea to book ahead via ⓦairporttaxi.is; the journey to Reykjavík takes around 45 minutes.

Airport buses are far cheaper than taxis, meet flights and run direct to Reykjavík (45min). Reykjavík Excursions (ⓦre.is) and Gray Line (ⓦgrayline.is) sell tickets in the arrivals terminal and take passengers either to their respective downtown terminuses or can offer drop-offs to accommodation. Keflanding (ⓦkeflanding.com) is the cheapest option, but you need to book online and it runs fewer services.

Reyjavík City Airport (RVK; ⓦisavia.is) is right on Reykjavík's southern outskirts and handles international flights from the Faroe Islands and Greenland, as well as domestic services from around the country. Catch Stræto bus #15 (5min) or a taxi (5min) into the city.

By ferry

The **Norröna International Ferry** (ⓦsmyril-line.com) runs a Denmark–Faroes–Iceland route. This is worth considering if you want to bring your own vehicle to Iceland, though you land right across the country at Seyðisfjörður, 675km from Reykjavík. One-way fares from Denmark are €565 per person for one vehicle and two people sleeping in a couchette; a private cabin costs around €100 more per person. If you arrive by ferry but without your own vehicle, first catch a local bus service to Egilsstaðir (45min) and then fly to Reykjavík (ⓦairiceland.is).

Getting around

Reykjavík's centre is so small that you can walk right across it in 30min, though city buses, bicycles and taxis come in handy for reaching some of the outlying sights and districts. For trips beyond the Greater Reykjavík area, you'll need to make use of long-distance buses, car rental or tours – and, just possibly, a flight.

City bus

Stræto (ⓦstraeto.is) operates a network of numbered city buses, with the main terminus just east of the city centre at **Hlemmur Square**. Services run Mon–Fri 6.35am–midnight, Sat 7.30am–midnight and Sun 9.30am–midnight; English-language timetables can be downloaded from its website.

Stopovers

Icelandair (ⓦicelandair.com) will allow a stopover in Iceland for up to seven nights at no extra cost to your transatlantic ticket.

Tickets must be bought on the bus (exact change only), with books of 20 tickets available. Alternatively, good-value one-day or three-day bus passes are available from newsagents around Hlemmur Square.

Taxi

Cabs are relatively inexpensive, and 3000–4000kr should get you across town; tipping is not expected. The main ranks are on Lækjargata; between Bankstræti and Amtmannsstígur; outside the Harpa concert hall; and in the vicinity of Hallgrímskirkja. For bookings, try Hreyfill (⊙ 588 5522, ⓦ hreyfill.is) or BSR (⊙ 561 0000, ⓦ bsr.is).

Bicycle

Reykjavík is comfortably scaled for riding a **bicycle** around, and you can also explore most of southern Iceland with a solid mountain bike or robust tourer. If you haven't brought your own along with you, bikes can be **rented** from some accommodation or from Reykjavík Bike Tours (ⓦ icelandbike. com), which also runs a range of guided trips. You should wear a helmet and weatherproof gear and, especially if you're venturing along some of the rougher roads outside the city, carry plenty of spares and a good-quality toolkit. In the countryside, it's also wise to bring more than enough food and water, as it can be a very long way between shops and settlements. If it all gets too much, put your bike **on a bus**.

Long-distance bus

Long-distance buses cover much of the country, but not all year round. The most comprehensive coverage is provided by **Strætó** (ⓦ straeto. is), whose long-distance terminus is at Mjódd, 4km southeast of the city centre (catch bus #11 from the city terminus at Hlemmur); it runs west

to various locations on Reykjanes, as well as east along the Ringroad to Vík. Ringroad destinations are also covered by **Reykjavík Experience** (ⓦ re.is), based at the BSÍ bus station, 500m south of the centre of town at Vatnsmýrarvegi 10, which also runs a bus to Geysir and Gullfoss; and **Sterna** (ⓦ sternatravel.com), whose main booking desk is located on Garðatorg 5, 210 Garðabær. For Interior destinations, **Trex** (ⓦ trex.is) operates daily from Reykjavík to Þórsmörk and Landmannalaugar, but only through the summer – roughly mid-June to early September.

Tickets for all these can be bought on the day, but it's best to book a couple of days in advance.

Car

For a short trip to Iceland, a **car** gives you the flexibility you need for exploring outside the capital and will get you to many places not covered by buses. **Rental costs** are competitive, especially if booked in advance or if you're visiting outside the June–September peak tourist season, when rates are lower. Companies either fix a daily maximum distance (say 100km) for the rental period, or allow unlimited mileage; **optional insurance** against windscreen damage, gravel damage, and how much of the **CDW** (Collision Damage Waiver) you'll be liable for, can double the daily rental cost.

A general-purpose **two- or four-door**, capable of handling all the main roads and the better gravel tracks, will cost around 15,000kr per day; a **camper van** will be at least 35,000kr a day (though you'll save on accommodation costs), while a **four-wheel-drive** – only advised if you have previous experience and want to reach Landmannalaugar or Þórsmörk under your own steam – costs upwards of 30,000kr.

Vehicles are left-hand drives, and you drive on the right. The speed limit is 50km/h in built-up areas, 90km/h on surfaced roads, and 80km/h on gravel. Seat belts are compulsory for all passengers, and headlights must be on at least half-beam all the time. **Road signs** include "Einbreið bru", indicating a single-lane bridge, and "Malbik endar", marking the end of a surfaced road. General warning signs are orange and marked "Varuð" or "Hætta" (warning or hazard).

Potential problems include having other vehicles spray you with windscreen-cracking gravel – so, when passing another car, slow down and pull over as far as possible, especially on unsurfaced roads. Outside the city, beware of the possibility of livestock wandering about. On gravel, or in snow and ice (unlikely during the summer), avoid skidding by keeping your speed down and applying the brakes slowly and as little as possible. In winter, rental vehicles are fitted with studded snow tyres, but you should carry food, water and a good blanket or sleeping bag in case your car gets stuck.

Flights

With the exception of the flight to Heimaey (see page 100), it's unlikely that you'll make use of Iceland's domestic airlines, Air Iceland (ⓦairiceland.is) and Eagle Air (ⓦeagleair.is) for transport. However, both also offer air tours over famous landscapes such as Hekla, Eyjafjallajökull, Þingvellir and Þórsmörk, lasting around 1hr 30min – check online for details.

Activities

Tours

Tours range from whale-watching cruises (see box, page 43) to guided hikes, pony treks (see page 125), cycle explorations of the city (see page 123), bus safaris and scenic sightseeing flights (see page 124). Some, like the popular Golden Circle tour that takes in Þingvellir, Geysir and Gullfoss, you can do independently without too much bother, but in other cases you'll find that organized tours are the only practical way of reaching an off-the-beaten-track destination.

The widest range is offered between June and September. In the October–May low season, the roads to Landmannalaugar and Þórsmörk will be impassable and operators concentrate on Northern Lights, four-wheel-driving and glacier exploration along the fringes of the southern ice caps. **Booking in advance** is always advisable to avoid disappointment, whatever the time of year.

Swimming

Swimming is a major social activity in Iceland and almost every settlement has an outdoor swimming pool, geothermally heated to 28°C, along with hot pots (hot tubs) at 35–40°C, and a sauna or steam room. Out in the wilds, hot pots are replaced by natural hot springs, such as those at Landmannalaugar. Apart from Laugardalslaug (see page 71), one of the most central pools in the city itself is the popular **Sundhöllin** at Barónsstígur 45A (ⓦitr.is; MAP PAGE 62, POCKET MAP H7), where there's a 25m indoor pool, an outdoor pool, two outdoor hot pots, plus single-sex nude sunbathing terraces.

When using an Icelandic swimming pool, take off your shoes before entering the changing rooms and leave them in the rack provided; leave your towel in the shower area between the changing rooms and the pool, not in your locker (so you can dry off before returning to the changing rooms); and shower fully, with soap and without swimwear, before getting in the pool.

Though there are always separate male and female changing rooms, very few pools have private cubicles.

Hiking

Southern Iceland is crossed by a web of **hiking trails**, the best known of which is the five-day Laugarvegur track between Landmannalaugar and Skógar via Þórsmörk (see box, page 109). But there are also plenty of much shorter hikes, lasting just a few hours, such as in the hills behind Hveragerði (see page 92) and various spots along the Reykjanes coast. Be aware, though, that even popular routes are seldom well marked; you'll always need to be competent at using navigational aids, especially in poor weather.

It's also prudent to seek local advice about routes, though many make light of difficulties: a "straightforward" hiking trail might involve traversing knife-edge ridges or dangerously loose scree slopes.

Always carry warm, weatherproof **clothing**, and wear tough hiking boots; being prepared means you can still get out and enjoy yourself in bad weather. You'll also need food and water, a torch, lighter, penknife, first-aid kit, a foil insulation blanket and a whistle or mirror for attracting attention; be sure to memorize Iceland's **emergency numbers** (see box, page 128). The prime hiking months are June through to August, when the weather is relatively warm, flowers are in bloom, and the wildlife is out and about – though, even then, you might experience snow inland.

Iceland has two main **hiking organizations**: Ferðafélag Íslands (Touring Club of Iceland; Mörkin 6, IS-108 Reykjavík, ⓦfi.is); and Útivist (Laugavegur 178, 105 Reykjavík, ⓦutivist.is). Contact one of them for general hiking information, group treks and to **book huts** at Landmannalaugar and Þórsmörk, and along Laugavegur.

Horseriding

Horses came to Iceland with the first Viking settlers, and have remained true to their original stocky Scandinavian breed. They're sturdy, even-tempered creatures and, in addition to the usual walk, trot, gallop and canter paces, can move smoothly across rough ground using the gliding *tölt* gait.

Horses are available for hire from farms right across southern Iceland, but to organize something in advance of your trip, check out Íshestar (ⓦishestar.is) or Eldhestar (ⓦeldhestar.is), which run treks lasting between an hour and several days for all experience levels.

Snow and action sports

There's not a huge enthusiasm for **skiing and snowboarding** in Iceland, perhaps because snow has generally been seen as just something you have to put up with. The main centre is around 20km from Reykjavík at **Bláfjöll** (ⓦskidasvaedi.is), where there are a few short slopes and a ski lift, though this is only open through the winter months.

Surprisingly, one of the world's greatest freshwater **scuba dives** is at Silfra near Þingvellir, featuring ice-blue water with truly stunning visibility. You need to be already certified and, ideally, have dry-suit skills; contact Dive Iceland (ⓦdive.is) or Dive Silfra (ⓦdivesilfra.is) for further details.

Directory A–Z

Accessible travel

Icelandic hotels are required by law to make a percentage of their rooms accessible. Transport – including ferries, airlines and some tour buses – can make provisions for wheelchair users if notified in advance.

Reykjavík's Disabled Association, Sjálfsbjörg, is at Hátún 12, 105 Reykjavík (ⓦ sjalfsbjorg.is, ⓔ sjalfsbjorg@sjalfsbjorg.is), and can advise on accessible accommodation and travel around Iceland. Download the Travable app to discover restaurants, pools and attractions based on their accessibility.

Addresses

Addresses in Iceland are given with the street name followed by the house number, post code and place i.e. "Hverfisgata 29, 101 Reykjavík".

Children

Reykjavík's supermarkets and pharmacies are well stocked with nappies and formula (though keep in mind where the next shops might be in the countryside). In bad weather, swimming pools – some of which have waterslides – make great places for children to let off steam. Be aware that special care needs to be taken at outdoor sites (see page 128).

Cinema

The multiplex Háskólabíó Cinema (Hagatorg, ⓦ smarabio.is; MAP PAGE 47, POCKET MAP M3), attached to the university, is Reykjavík's main picture house. It screens mainstream film productions and is the only cinema in the country with Dolby Digital 3D.

Crime

Reykjavík is a relatively safe place with low levels of crime, most of it opportunistic: don't walk around the downtown area alone late at night, or leave valuables lying about or on show in a parked car, and you'll have few problems. The police (*lögrelan*) are English-speaking, unarmed and keen to help, should you need them; for general information dial ☎ 444 1000 or, in an **emergency**, ☎ 112.

Electricity

Electricity is 240v, 50Hz AC. Plugs and sockets are two-pin round prongs; make sure you carry an adaptor.

Embassies & consulates

Canada Túngata 14, 101 Reykjavík ☎ 575 6500, ⓦ canadainternational. gc.ca; **China** Borgartún 6, 105 Reykjavík ☎ 527 6688, ⓦ china-embassy.is; **Denmark** Hverfisgata 29, 101 Reykjavík ☎ 575 0300, ⓦ island.um.dk; **Finland** Túngata 30, 101 Reykjavík ☎ 510 0100, ⓦ finland.is; **France** Túngata 22, 101 Reykjavík ☎ 575 9600, ⓦ ambafrance. is; **Germany** Laufásvegur 31, 101 Reykjavík ☎ 530 1100, ⓦ reykjavik. diplo.de; **Greenland** Hverfisgata 29, 101 Reykjavík ☎ 575 0300, ⓦ island. um.dk; **Norway** Fjólugata 17, 101 Reykjavík ☎ 520 0700, ⓦ noregur. is; **Sweden** Lágmúli 7 ☎ 520 1230, ⓦ swedenabroad.com; **UK** Laufásvegur 31, 101 Reykjavík ☎ 550 5100 ⓦ britishembassy.is; **USA** Laufásvegur 21, 101 Reykjavík ☎ 595 2200, ⓦ is.usembassy.gov.

Health

Reykjavík's health services are modern and efficient, and all doctors will speak English. No vaccinations are required for visitors to Iceland. Water is safe to drink everywhere.

In an **emergency**, dial ☎ 112 or get to Landspitali Emergency Department,

Fossvogur, 108 Reykjavík (open 24hr; pocket map N3). For less urgent treatment, Reykjavík has fifteen medical centres (*heilsugaeslan*); your accommodation can contact one for you, or there's a list available at Ⓦ heilsugaeslan.is/stadsetning.

For free healthcare treatment, Scandinavian citizens must show medical insurance and a valid passport, while citizens of the European Economic Area need their European Health Insurance Card and passport. Otherwise, you'll need to pay at the time and then claim back the money from travel insurance.

For **emergency dental treatment** only, contact Tannlaeknavaktin at Skipholt 33 (Mon–Fri 8am–10pm, Sat & Sun 10am–8pm; Ⓣ426 8000, Ⓦtannlaeknavaktin.is), which is around a twenty-minute walk east of Hallgrímskirkja.

There are no 24hr **pharmacies** (*apotek*) in Reykjavík, but one of the longest-opening is Lyfja at Lágmúli 5, 108 Reykjavík (daily 8am–midnight; Ⓣ533 2300). It's located around 2km east of Hallgrímskirkja.

Internet

Iceland is one of the highest per-capita users of the internet. Most Reykjavík cafés and accommodation provide free wi-fi for customers, and getting connected is seldom a problem in the city.

Left luggage

If your accommodation can't store luggage for you, there are lockers at the BSÍ bus station, Vatnsmýrarvegi 10 (open 24hr; maximum three days); the Reykjavík City Airport terminal (open 30min before first flight in the morning and closes 30min after last arrival in the evening; maximum thirty days); and at Keflavík International Airport (daily 5am–5pm; maximum thirty days).

LGBTQ+ travellers

Given that Iceland is a fairly liberal country – former prime minister Jóhanna Sigurðardóttir was the world's first openly lesbian head of government – there's little discrimination and, consequently, no specifically gay venues in Reykjavík. For listings check out Ⓦgayice.is, or for general information contact the Icelandic LGBTQ+ association, Samtökin 78 (Suðurgata 3, Reykjavík Ⓦsamtokin78.is).

Money

Icelandic krónur (Isk, Ikr or kr) come in 5000kr, 2000kr, 1000kr and 500kr notes, with 100kr, 50kr, 10kr, 5kr and 1kr coins. There are plenty of banks with ATMs in central Reykjavík and larger towns; you can also find ATMs at some country fuel stations. However, you can pay for almost anything in Iceland using bank debit or credit cards (Visa and Mastercard are the most widely accepted), and it's quite feasible to spend a week here without using cash – except on Strætó buses (see page 122).

Opening hours

Generally, business hours are Monday to Friday 10am–6pm and Saturday 10am until mid-afternoon; if they open on Sunday, it will probably be after noon. In Reykjavík and larger towns, supermarkets open daily from 10am until late afternoon; in smaller communities, however, some places don't open at all at weekends. Country fuel stations provide some services for travellers, and larger ones tend to open daily 9am–10pm. Office hours are Monday to Friday 9am–5pm.

Phones

Icelandic phone numbers are seven digits long, with no area codes. Phone directories are ordered by Christian name – Jakob Gunnarsson,

Emergency numbers

In an emergency, dial ☎ 112 for fire, ambulance or police.

for example, would be listed under J, not G. Landline rates are cheapest for domestic calls at weekends and 7pm–8am Monday–Friday; on calls to Europe daily 7pm–8am; and to everywhere else daily 11pm–8am.

Iceland uses both GSM and NMT (Nordic Mobile Telephone) mobile phone networks. GSM covers Reykjavík and almost all the surrounding region; coming from the UK or EU, your own country's pay-as-you-go SIM cards might work with varying roaming rates, or buy a new pay-as-you-go SIM from fuel stations or newsagents in Iceland.

You'll only need NMT coverage for remoter interior regions; contact Icelandic car rental companies or hiking organizations (see page 125) for more information.

Post

Post offices are open Monday to Friday 9am–4.30pm, though a few in Reykjavík have longer hours. Domestic mail takes around two working days; count on three to five days for mail to reach the UK or US, and a week to ten days to reach Australia and New Zealand. For parcel rates, check ⓦ postur.is.

Price codes

Accommodation (see box, page 112) and eating out listings (see box, below) throughout the Guide have been categorized according to a price code, which correspond to price ranges.

Safety

You need to be responsible for your own safety in Iceland; there are so many natural hazards that it is impossible to fence them all off, and you shouldn't expect to find warning signs, safety barriers or guide ropes even at extremely dangerous locations, such as the edge of waterfalls, volcanoes or boiling mud pits.

The summer sun is strong, especially when reflected off ice or snow, so use sunscreen and wear sunglasses. Moisturizer and lip balm help protect against cold dry air, wind and dust.

Hypothermia – when your core body temperature drops dangerously – occurs if you get simultaneously exhausted, wet and cold; symptoms include a weak pulse, disorientation, numbness and slurred speech. Treatment involves getting as dry and as warm as possible, and taking sugary drinks. Serious cases need

Eating out price codes

Throughout the Guide, eating out listings are categorized according to a price code, which roughly corresponds to the following price ranges. Price categories reflect the cost of a two-course meal for one, without alcohol (which is very expensive in Iceland).

Kr	under 5000kr
KrKr	5000–7000kr
KrKrKr	7000–9000kr
KrKrKrKr	over 9000kr

Safe travel

If you're planning to hike, cycle or drive into Iceland's remoter corners, sign up first with ⓦ safetravel.is. The website provides alerts for hiking trail and highland road conditions, plus advice on how to prepare for your trip, and allows you to leave a travel plan and contact information with them, which will be followed up if you fail to report back at the appointed time.

In case of an emergency, **call 112**. For those with smartphones, there's also a free **112 app** available, which, when activated, transmits your location and nominated contact information to the rescue services.

hospital treatment. Avoid hypothermia by eating sufficient carbohydrates, drinking plenty of water and wearing warm and weatherproof clothing.

Smoking
Smoking is banned indoors in public buildings, restaurants, bars and cafés, and on school grounds, sport facilities or public areas of apartment buildings. Smoking is also prohibited inside most accommodation. You need to be at least 18 years old to purchase cigarettes, which are only sold by convenience stores and a few bars.

Tax refunds
If you spend more than 6000kr in any single transaction on goods to take out of the country, you are entitled to a tax refund of fifteen percent of the total price, as long as you leave Iceland within ninety days. Ask for a **Refund Tax Free form** when you make your purchases, which needs to be filled out by the shop. Money can be refunded in full back onto

your credit/debit card at refund points located in the departure halls at Keflavík and Reykjavík airports; on board all international cruise ships two hours before departure; or at Reykjavík port's Visitor Centre. The same places, plus refund points at Kringlan shopping centre and Reykjavík's Tourist Information centres, can make the refund in cash, but this incurs a commission.

Time
Iceland is on Greenwich Mean Time (GMT) year-round. GMT is five hours ahead of US Eastern Standard Time and ten hours behind Australian Eastern Standard Time.

Tipping
Tipping is not expected anywhere in Iceland, including for service in hotels, restaurants and taxis.

Tourist information
The **Reykjavík Tourist Office** has two What's On? information centres located in the heart of the city (at

Weather and road conditions

Keep up to speed with English-language **weather forecasts** at ⓦ en.vedur.is, which gives appraisals for the week ahead. If you're travelling around outside of Reykjavík, check up-to-the-minute **road conditions** at ⓦ road.is, with online access to cameras and colour-coded maps.

Laugavegur 5 and 54; ☏590 1550, ⓦvisitreykjavik.is). It is a useful source of information for local events, and can also help organize or advise about tours, accommodation and car rental. It's also worth checking out **Reykjavík Grapevine** (ⓦgrapevine.is), an irreverent weekly listings magazine which reviews attractions, parties, bands, restaurants and upcoming events in the city.

Festivals and events

Though Iceland's calendar is essentially Christian, many official holidays and festivals have a secular theme.

Þorrablót

February
A midwinter feast once honouring the Viking weather god Þorri. Today, people eat traditional foods such as *svið* (sheep's head) and *hákarl* (fermented shark).

Bjórdagur (Beer Day)

March 1
Festival honouring the date in 1989 that Iceland's 74-year-old prohibition on beer was lifted. Best experienced by joining in a *rúntur* (bar crawl).

Sjomannadagur (Seamen's Day)

June 4
Expect mock sea-rescue demonstrations, swimming races and tug-of-war battles, especially around Reykjavík's old harbour.

Independence Day

June 17
The day the Icelandic state separated from Denmark in 1944. Low-key events held in central Reykjavík.

Jónsmessa

June 24
Magical creatures are said to be out in force, playing tricks on the unwary. Some people celebrate with a big bonfire; others roll around naked in the morning dew.

Verslunnarmannahelgi (Labour Day Weekend)

First weekend in August
Traditionally, everybody heads into the countryside, sets up camp, and parties themselves into oblivion.

Þjódhátið

First weekend in August
Held inside an extinct volcano crater on Heimaey (see page 100), and celebrated in much the same spirit as Labour Day on the mainland. Be sure to

Public holiday dates

Jan 1 New Year's Day
March/April Maundy Thursday, Good Friday, Easter Sunday, Easter Monday
April, first Thursday after April 18 First day of summer
May 1 May Day
May/June Ascension Day, Whit Sunday, Whit Monday
June 17 National Day
August Bank Holiday (first Monday)
Dec 24–26 Christmas Eve, Christmas Day, Boxing Day
Dec 31 New Year's Eve

book transport and accommodation a year in advance.

Rettir

Autumn

The *rettir*, or stock round-up, takes place in Iceland's rural areas throughout the month of September. Horses and sheep are herded from the higher summer pastures to be penned; some farms allow visitors to watch or even participate.

Chronology

16 million years ago As the Eurasian and North American tectonic plates begin to tear apart, Iceland first pops out of the waves during volcanic eruptions.

300 BC Historian Pytheas of Marseille writes about a frozen Arctic land named "Ultima Thule", possibly Iceland.

c.800 AD Christian monks from Ireland settle the southern coast.

c.850 A Viking adventurer named Naddoddur accidentally discovers Iceland.

874 Norwegian-born Ingólfur Arnarson settles the area of Reykjavík ("Smoky Bay"), becoming the country's first known resident.

870–930 Vikings, mostly from Norway, colonize all Iceland during the Landnám, or Settlement Period.

930 Iceland declares itself a Commonwealth, with an annual parliament held at Þingvellir.

980–1000 Vikings discover Greenland and North America.

1000 Christianity becomes Iceland's national religion.

1104 Hekla volcano erupts violently, burying farms across the south of the country.

1220–62 The "Sturlung Age" ushers in a period of civil war; many of Iceland's historic sagas are written down, extolling the virtues of earlier times.

1262 The "Old Treaty" cedes Icelandic sovereignty to Norway, ending the civil war.

1280 The *Jónsbók* of laws is compiled.

1397 The Kalmar Union sees Norway, and hence Iceland, brought under Danish rule.

1402 Plague arrives in Iceland; almost half the population dies.

1420–1532 Denmark, England and Germany tussle over Icelandic trading rights during the "English Century".

1550 As the Reformation sweeps Europe, Iceland's last Catholic bishop, Jón Arason, is executed at Skálholt and the country becomes Lutheran.

1602 Denmark imposes a repressive trade monopoly on Iceland, beggaring the country and reducing the population to the status of tenant farmers.

1752 Bailif Skúli Magnússon founds an Icelandic trading company, whose warehouses at Reykjavík become the core of Iceland's first town.

1783 Poisonous fallout from the gigantic Lakí eruptions in eastern

Iceland sterilizes farms across the country, causing famines and killing a third of the population.

1787 Denmark lifts the trade monopoly.

1835 Jónas Hallgrímsson (and later Jón Sigurðsson) champions the idea of Icelandic nationalism and independence from Denmark.

1843 The Danish king approves reconstitution of the Alþing at Reykjavík.

1871 Denmark annexes Iceland.

1904 Home Rule: Denmark grants political independence to Iceland.

1918 Iceland becomes an independent Danish state.

1940–45 During World War II, British and US forces occupy Iceland. After Denmark is captured by the Nazis, Iceland declares itself fully independent on June 17, 1944.

1949–51 As the Cold War gains momentum, Iceland joins NATO and the US opens an airbase at Keflavík.

1958–85 Iceland gradually expands its territorial waters to a two-hundred-mile (320km) radius around the country, sparking a series of "Cod Wars" with Britain over fishing rights.

1994 Iceland becomes part of Europe, but stops short of joining the EU.

1998–2008 Unregulated attempts to diversify the economy away from fishing by investing in banking creates a financial bubble which implodes in 2008, leaving twenty percent of Icelanders bankrupt.

2010 The Eyjafjallajökull volcano erupts in a mighty ash cloud, causing aviation chaos in Europe – and bringing Iceland's raw landscape to the attention of international tourism.

2011–2018 Tourist numbers grow twenty percent annually, reaching nearly two million visitors in 2018 – compared with a national population of just 331,000. Tourism becomes the biggest single source of revenue.

2021–2022 Volcano erupts south of the capital in the Geldingadalur valley in March 2021 and lasts six months – the first eruption in eight centuries. Another volcano eruption in August 2022, this time in the Meradalir valley, lasting three weeks.

2023 A string of earthquakes is followed by a volcano eruption in the Reykjanes Peninsula, though no damage to local communities or infrastructure.

Language

Icelandic is a medieval language, retaining much of the complex grammar that has largely dropped out of use elsewhere in Europe. And while you might even recognize a few dialect nouns – tjörn for tarn (small pond), fjall for fell (mountain) – the pronunciation will leave you reeling (fjall is pronounced "fyatl", for example). Fortunately most Icelanders speak **English**, alongside other Nordic languages and a smattering of French and German; as they don't expect foreigners to know a word of Icelandic you'll delight everyone by attempting even the simplest phrase.

There are **32 letters** in the Icelandic alphabet, including Þ (þ) and Ð (ð)

– both, to all intents and purposes, pronounced "th". Bizarrely, there is no exact Icelandic equivalent for the word "interesting" – the closest being *gaman*, fun.

An idea of pronunciation is given in brackets where useful.

Basic words and phrases

I don't understand ég skil ekki (yairg skil ekee)

Could you speak more slowly? gætirðu talað hægar? (gye-tiroo talath hyegar)

Do you speak English? talarðu ensku? (talarthoo enskoo)

Yes já (yau)

No nei (nay)

Hello hæ (hi)

Good morning/afternoon góðan dag (go-than dargh)

Good night góða nótt (go-tha not)

Goodbye bless

Please afsakið (afsakith)

Thank you takk fyrir

What's your name? hvað heitirðu? (kvath haytiroo?)

I'd like... ég ætla að fá (yairg aytla ath fau)

Excuse me fyrirgefðu (fyrir gef thoo)

How much does it cost? hvað kostar þetta? (kvath kostar thetta?)

Where hvar (kvar)

Toilet snyrting

Men/women karlmenn/kvenmenn

Open/closed opið/lokað (opith/ lokath)

Bill/check, please reikninginn, takk

Food and drink

arctic char bleikja

beer bjór

bread brauð

burger hamborgari

butter smjör

cheese ostur

cod þorskur

coffee kaffi

egg egg

fermented shark hákarl

fish fiskur

herring sild

hot dog pylsur

Icelandic vodka brennivín

Icelandic yoghurt skyr

lamb lamb

lobster humar

milk mjólk

pancakes, flatbread laufabrauð, flatbrauð

pepper pipar

pizza pítsa

ptarmigan rjúpa

reindeer hreindýr

salmon lax

salt salt

skimmed milk lettmjólk

smoked lamb hangikjöt

soup súpa

"steam bread" hverabrauð

sugar sykur

tea te

trout silungur

water vatn

wind-dried cod harðifiskur

SMALL PRINT

Publishing Information
Third edition 2024

Distribution
UK, Ireland and Europe
Apa Publications (UK) Ltd; sales@roughguides.com
United States and Canada
Ingram Publisher Services; ips@ingramcontent.com
Australia and New Zealand
Booktopia; retailer@booktopia.com.au
Worldwide
Apa Publications (UK) Ltd; sales@roughguides.com

Special Sales, Content Licensing and CoPublishing
Rough Guides can be purchased in bulk quantities at discounted prices. We can create special editions, personalised jackets and corporate imprints tailored to your needs. sales@roughguides.com.
roughguides.com

Printed in Czech Republic

This book was produced using **Typefi** automated publishing software.

A catalogue record for this book is available from the British Library

The publishers and authors have done their best to ensure the accuracy and currency of all the information in **Pocket Rough Guide Reykjavík**, however, they can accept no responsibility for any loss, injury, or inconvenience sustained by any traveller as a result of information or advice contained in the guide.

Rough Guide Credits
Editor: Joanna Reeves
Cartography: Carte
Picture Editor: Piotr Kala
Head of Pictures: Tom Smyth
Layout: Pradeep Thapliyal
Original design: Richard Czapnik
Head of DTP and Pre-Press: Rebeka Davies
Head of Publishing: Sarah Clark

About the author

Joanna Reeves is a Sussex-based travel writer and editor for whom Reykjavík holds a special place in her heart. She has updated several Rough Guides, including the *Rough Guide to England*, *Pocket Rough Guide Porto* and *Rough Guide Mini Bologna*. She is also the editor of the brand-new *Rough Guide to Slow Travel in Europe*.

Help us update

We've gone to a lot of effort to ensure that this edition of the **Pocket Rough Guide Reykjavík** is accurate and up-to-date. However, things change – places get "discovered", opening hours are notoriously fickle, restaurants and rooms raise prices or lower standards. If you feel we've got it wrong or left something out, we'd like to know, and if you can remember the address, the price, the hours, the phone number, so much the better.

Please send your comments with the subject line "**Pocket Rough Guide Reykjavík Update**" to mail@uk.roughguides.com. We'll credit all contributions and send a copy of the next edition (or any other Rough Guide if you prefer) for the very best emails.

Photo Credits

(Key: T-top; C-centre; B-bottom; L-left; R-right)

All images **Shutterstock** except the following:

A.Currell 31
Alyson Hurt 103
DaseinDesign 51
fotoVoyager 60
Helgi Halldórsson 50
Helgi Halldórsson 37B
Jennifer Boyer 101
Karl Petersson 21B
Neverse/Dreamstime.com 109

Reykjavík Art Museum / Vigfús Birgisson 69T
Rough Guides 2C, 12/13B, 15B, 16B, 17B, 18T, 18C, 18B, 19T, 19B, 21T, 21C, 24/25, 26, 29, 32, 35, 37T, 38B, 39T, 40, 42T, 42B, 44, 45, 46, 48, 52, 53, 56, 57T, 57B, 62, 64, 65, 66, 68, 69B, 71, 75, 78, 79, 80, 86, 88, 91B, 92, 93B, 106B

Cover Winter skyline **Patpong Sirikul/Shutterstock**

Index

NOTES

NOTES

NOTES